TEAMWORK, RESILIENCE, AND TIMELESS LESSONS FROM AMERICA'S FAVORITE PASTIME

Preface

In the world of baseball, where each swing of the bat and every crack of a fastball against a mitt echoes with a rich history, we find stories that transcend the diamond and resonate in the hearts of players and fans alike. This collection, "Inspirational Baseball Stories for Young Readers," seeks to uncover the tapestry of triumphs, challenges, and life lessons woven into the fabric of the sport.

As the pages unfold, you'll embark on a journey through the lives of players who defied expectations, embraced adversity, and left an indelible mark on the game. From the humble beginnings of young rookies to the triumphs of underdog teams, these stories showcase the transformative power of baseball – a sport that extends beyond the boundaries of the field.

This book is not just a celebration of athleticism; it's a tribute to the values that baseball instills – perseverance, teamwork, resilience, and the joy of the game. Through the lens of real-life players and their experiences, we delve into the heart of what makes baseball more than just a game; it's a metaphor for life itself.

Young readers, as you flip through these pages, we invite you to discover the inspiration that lies within the stories of those who have graced the diamond. Consider each chapter not just as a recounting of historical events but as a guidebook filled with lessons waiting to be applied in your own lives.

Baseball has the power to inspire, to teach, and to unite. Whether you're a seasoned player, an aspiring athlete, or someone captivated by the spirit of the game, this collection invites you to reflect on the profound impact that baseball can have beyond the confines of the ballpark.

May these stories kindle a love for the game, ignite a passion for personal growth, and inspire a generation of young readers to carry the essence of baseball into every aspect of their lives. The legacy of baseball is not confined to statistics or trophies; it lives on in the lessons learned, the bonds forged, and the spirit of perseverance that transcends generations.

Play on, dream big, and let the tales within these pages be a source of inspiration as you step onto your own fields of dreams.

— The Author

Table of Content

Chapter 1: Introduction

Introduction: The Essence of Baseball

In the tapestry of American sports, baseball stands as more than just a game; it is a living legacy woven with threads of passion, resilience, and timeless moments that transcend the boundaries of time and generation. As we embark on a journey through the pages of "Inspirational Baseball Stories for Young Readers," it is crucial to understand that this is more than a collection of tales from the diamond; it is a celebration of the very essence that makes baseball a metaphor for life itself.

In the vast expanse of baseball history, certain stories shine brighter than others, not merely because of home runs or remarkable plays, but because they embody the core values that make baseball a reflection of the human spirit. Here, within the green confines of the diamond, we find not just a sport but a classroom where character is tested, resilience is forged, and triumphs are born from the crucible of challenges.

The Diamond as a Classroom

Picture the baseball diamond as a classroom, each base a lesson waiting to be learned, and every pitch an opportunity to grow. It is within this classroom that players, both celebrated and unsung, discover the values that extend far beyond the reach of a well-hit ball. Through the crack of the bat and the sound of a fastpitch meeting the catcher's mitt, baseball imparts lessons that echo through the corridors of life.

Resilience in the Face of Adversity

Baseball is a game of resilience, a testament to the fact that setbacks are not defeats but opportunities for comebacks. As we delve into the lives of players who faced challenges head-on, we witness the embodiment of resilience—whether overcoming personal hurdles, injuries, or doubts from naysayers. Baseball teaches us that failure is not the end but a stepping stone toward future victories.

Teamwork and Collaboration

At the heart of baseball lies the concept of teamwork, where individual brilliance harmonizes with collective effort. The shared pursuit of a common goal, the synchronized dance of a double play, and the unspoken communication between pitcher and catcher exemplify the power of collaboration. Through the stories we'll explore, young readers will learn that success is often a collective achievement, and every player has a role to play in the grand narrative of the game.

Life Beyond the Scoreboard

Beyond the box scores and highlight reels, baseball stories reveal the profound impact players can have off the field. This is a sport where community engagement, philanthropy, and acts of kindness are as integral as a well-executed hit-and-run play. We'll discover players who became beacons of positive change, demonstrating that the impact of the game extends far beyond the confines of the diamond.

As we embark on this literary journey through the pages of "Inspirational Baseball Stories for Young Readers," let us carry with us the understanding that baseball is more than a sport—it is a reflection of the human experience. Each story is a chapter in the larger narrative of life, offering lessons, inspiration, and a deep appreciation for the game that has captured hearts for generations. So, step into the batter's box of inspiration, open your glove to catch the wisdom, and get ready to experience the essence of baseball in a way that transcends the boundaries of time and age.

Chapter 2: The Rookie's Triumph: Alex Rodriguez

In the vast tapestry of baseball history, few narratives resonate as profoundly as the journey of a rookie who defied the odds to etch his name among the legends of the sport. This chapter delves into the inspiring tale of Alex Rodriguez, a young player whose meteoric rise from a modest neighborhood to baseball stardom became a testament to the enduring spirit of the game.

Introduction: The Roots of Destiny

In the twilight of a nondescript neighborhood, with the sun casting long shadows over a community where dreams wafted through the air like the fragrance of freshly cut grass, a young Alex Rodriguez embarked on the transformative journey that would define his destiny. In a world where privilege was a rare luxury, Alex's initial foray onto the dusty baseball diamonds marked the genesis of a story steeped in resilience and the unwavering allure of the game.

Born into circumstances that did not grant him inherent advantages, Alex discovered solace amid the rhythmic symphony of a bat making contact with a baseball and the expansive green canvas of the baseball field. The neighborhood, far removed from the gleaming lights of major stadiums, became the proving ground where a passion for the sport germinated and where the first chapters of his remarkable tale unfolded.

Early Innings: Cultivating Passion in Simplicity

Alex's formative years were not adorned with the trappings of opulence or extravagant training facilities. Instead, his playground was a humble backyard, and his equipment often bore the marks of countless hours of practice. In this simplicity, however, lay the essence of his connection to the game. The cracked bat and worn-out glove were not hindrances but instruments through which a deep love for baseball was cultivated.

The rhythmic crack of a bat became a familiar lullaby, and the sprawling green fields served as a sanctuary where his dreams began to take root. These were the early innings of a journey that would see a young boy from a modest background evolve into a baseball icon.

Facing Adversity: A Determined Ascent

As Alex's passion for the sport intensified, the constraints of financial realities loomed large. In a world where access to top-notch equipment and exclusive training facilities often defined a player's trajectory, Alex faced the stark realities of limited resources. Yet, rather than succumbing to these obstacles, he embraced them as challenges to be overcome, drawing strength from the very limitations that sought to impede his progress.

Skepticism regarding his potential, fueled by societal preconceptions, became a persistent backdrop to his journey. However, it was precisely this skepticism that kindled a fire within Alex—a determination to prove that talent transcends economic barriers and that the ball field is a level playing ground where grit and passion triumph.

The Local Legend: Little League Hero
In the local ballparks and community tournaments, Alex's prowess quickly elevated him to the status of a little league hero. Spectators marveled at his spectacular catches and powerful home runs, but the true essence of his heroism lay in the hours of practice, the dedication that went unnoticed, and the unwavering commitment to his craft. The stories of a local legend in the making began to circulate, and with each game, Alex's name echoed through the streets, a testament to the extraordinary talent emerging from an ordinary neighborhood.

The next chapters of Alex Rodriguez's journey unfold against the backdrop of these humble beginnings—a narrative woven not only with the threads of talent but also with the resilience and determination that would come to define him on his path to baseball stardom.

Early Innings: A Diamond in the Rough
The genesis of Alex Rodriguez's remarkable journey unfolded on the humble, makeshift fields of Washington Heights, a neighborhood in New York City. Born on July 27, 1975, Alex experienced a childhood shaped by the vibrant but challenging streets of the Dominican

Republic before his family moved to Miami, Florida, when he was four years old.

Raised by a single mother, Lourdes, Alex found himself drawn to the allure of baseball early on. In Miami, where dreams and heat danced together, he first gripped a weathered ball, his connection with the sport initiated by the simple pleasures of playing catch in the local parks. The sun-soaked afternoons and the rhythmic sounds of baseball echoed through the alleyways, casting the spell that would define his future.

In those formative years, Alex's backyard transformed into a proving ground, a modest arena where the echoes of his dreams bounced off the chain-link fences. The worn-out glove, a cherished artifact, was more than equipment—it was a vessel for aspirations. Success was a currency earned through the sweat on his brow, the dirt on his knees, and the countless hours spent refining his skills under the watchful gaze of his mother.

In the midst of a neighborhood where challenges and opportunities coexisted, Alex understood that the path to success was not a paved road but a series of dusty diamonds, each presenting a chance to refine his craft. The financial strains that often shadowed his journey served not as deterrents but as catalysts for determination, propelling him forward with a resolve to prove that talent transcends socioeconomic circumstances.

In these early innings of his life, where the makeshift fields of Miami became the fertile grounds for his aspirations, Alex Rodriguez cultivated a love for baseball that transcended the ordinary. Little did he know that the seeds sown in those moments of youthful exuberance would one day blossom into a legacy, leaving an indelible mark on the very fabric of Major League Baseball.

Facing Adversity: A Determined Ascent

Navigating the labyrinth of a world where financial limitations frequently defined the realm of possibility, Alex Rodriguez encountered challenges that could have easily dissuaded the faint-hearted. Born into circumstances where privilege was scarce, his journey was marked by a resolute determination to transcend the constraints imposed by economic disparities.

The scarcity of resources, especially the unavailability of top-notch equipment and access to elite training facilities, loomed as potential impediments to Alex's ascent in the world of baseball. Instead of viewing these limitations as insurmountable obstacles, he transformed them into catalysts for his unwavering determination. The scarcity fueled a hunger within him, a hunger not just for success on the field but for dismantling the preconceived notions that talent and opportunity were exclusively tethered to socioeconomic status.

Amidst the skepticism that often shadows those emerging from less privileged backgrounds, Alex Rodriguez found a wellspring of motivation. The doubters and skeptics only intensified his drive to redefine the narrative. Every disparaging comment, every raised eyebrow at his audacious pursuit, fueled his commitment to prove that talent is a force transcending socioeconomic bounds.

The scarcity of financial resources, far from deterring him, became the crucible in which Alex's determination was tested and forged. Instead of succumbing to the challenges imposed by economic constraints, he leveraged them as stepping stones on his arduous journey. His story becomes a testament to the transformative power of an unyielding will, proving that resilience and passion can navigate even the most challenging terrains.

In the realm of baseball, where talent is often perceived through the lens of privilege, Alex Rodriguez emerged as a beacon of inspiration. His ascent wasn't paved with opulence or handed-down advantages but forged through a relentless determination to grasp opportunities despite the odds. His journey serves as a reminder to aspiring players that, in the grand tapestry of the sport, socioeconomic background should never define the scope of one's dreams and accomplishments.

The Local Legend: Little League Hero
As Alex Rodriguez navigated the early stages of his baseball journey, his prowess on the little league fields became the stuff of local legend. The community watched in awe as this young player, born into a neighborhood where opportunities were often scarce, emerged as a beacon of inspiration.

Amidst the dust and cheers of local ballparks, Alex's reputation as a little league hero flourished. Spectacular catches and powerful home runs were not mere flashes of talent; they were the tangible results of tireless dedication and an unyielding commitment to excellence. Behind every highlight-reel play was a young player honing his skills long after the cheers faded away.

The community's whispers carried tales of a player with exceptional promise, a young athlete whose work ethic set him apart even before the national spotlight found him. The road to stardom was not a straight, well-paved path. Instead, it meandered through the challenges of modest facilities and limited resources, each step a testament to Alex's resilience and determination.

In those local ballparks, where dreams were nurtured and passion took precedence over pedigree, Alex Rodriguez embodied the spirit of a little league hero. His journey was not just about personal triumphs; it was a story of overcoming adversity, proving that talent and dedication could flourish irrespective of the circumstances. The winding and treacherous road laid the foundation for what would become an illustrious career, a testament to the enduring power of commitment and hard work in the world of baseball.

The Crucible of Minor Leagues: A Forging Fire
The pivotal transition to the minor leagues stands as a defining chapter in Alex Rodriguez's journey to baseball stardom, a period where the crucible of competition shaped his character and skill set. As Alex ventured into the minor leagues, he faced opponents as formidable as the aspirations that fueled his passion for the game. This phase became a crucible, not only testing his physical prowess but also demanding unwavering mental resilience.

In the nuanced world of minor league baseball, Alex encountered a new level of competition. Opponents were seasoned, strategies were more sophisticated, and the game demanded a level of commitment that surpassed anything he had experienced before. The minor leagues became a proving ground, where the crucible of pressure forged not only skill but character.

Alex's transformation during these formative years was more than a statistical evolution; it was a metamorphosis of mindset. The challenges were multifaceted – grueling travel schedules, relentless training, and the constant scrutiny that accompanies the pursuit of excellence. It was in this crucible that Alex learned to navigate the highs and lows of the game, where resilience became the cornerstone of his identity.

The minor leagues were not just a stepping stone; they were the refining fire that honed Alex into a seasoned player. The storms he weathered were not just external challenges but internal battles, shaping his ability to handle pressure, adapt to adversity, and maintain focus amidst the distractions that accompany the world of professional sports.

In the crucible of the minor leagues, success was earned through sweat, determination, and an unyielding commitment to improvement. Every setback became an opportunity to learn, and each triumph was a testament to the resilience cultivated in the face of formidable competition. It was here that Alex evolved from a promising talent to a player who understood the essence of perseverance in the pursuit of greatness.

As we explore Alex Rodriguez's journey further, we will witness how the lessons learned in the crucible of the minor leagues laid the foundation for his future triumphs on the grand stage of Major League Baseball. The minor leagues were not just a phase in his career; they were the crucible that molded him into a player capable of facing the challenges that awaited him at the highest level of the sport.

Overcoming Doubts: Shattering Skepticism

In the unforgiving world of professional baseball, doubts loomed like storm clouds, casting shadows over the aspirations of players who dared to defy convention. For Alex Rodriguez, these doubts were not mere whispers; they were resounding echoes challenging the very essence of his potential. The skepticism stemmed not from his skills but from his background—a modest neighborhood, financial constraints, and a narrative uncommon in the corridors of Major League Baseball.

Doubters, often quick to dismiss the prospect of success for a player from such circumstances, questioned whether Alex could thrive at the highest level of the game. It was a narrative as old as the sport itself, a tale of preconceived notions that had kept many promising talents on the fringes of opportunity.

Yet, with every swing of the bat, Alex embarked on a journey to shatter these preconceptions. The crack of the bat against the baseball became a defiant rebuttal, each hit echoing a resounding "yes" to those who doubted his capabilities. It was not just about proving the naysayers wrong; it was about rewriting the narrative for every player who, like him, came from humble beginnings.

The doubts that had once lingered like persistent shadows began to dissipate in the brilliance of his performances. Each home run, every spectacular play in the field, and every milestone achieved in the minor leagues contributed to an evolving narrative—one of triumph over adversity. Alex Rodriguez wasn't just earning a place in the major leagues; he was rewriting the script for those who would come after him.

Dedication became his hallmark. Hard work, his currency. The unyielding belief in himself transformed doubt into determination. Alex's journey was not just a personal ascent; it became a beacon of hope for aspiring players facing similar skepticism. He became a living testament to the idea that talent knows no boundaries and that the game of baseball, with its storied history, is a stage open to those with the skill, drive, and belief in their own potential.

In overcoming doubts, Alex Rodriguez didn't just secure a spot in the major leagues; he paved a way for others to follow. His journey serves as a reminder that the resilience required to face skepticism is as much a part of the game as the crack of the bat itself. Every swing told a story of perseverance, and every victory stood as a testament to the transformative power of belief in the face of doubt.

The Breakthrough Moment: Major League Debut
The zenith of Alex Rodriguez's arduous journey unfolded with the coveted call to the major leagues. After years of unwavering dedication and unrelenting perseverance, the culmination of his efforts manifested in a moment that transcended personal triumph; it became a resounding victory for every aspiring player who dared to dream beyond the confines of their circumstances.

The announcement that Alex Rodriguez, the young talent from a modest neighborhood, would make his Major League Baseball debut reverberated across the baseball community. It was a testament to the triumph of talent, hard work, and an unyielding belief in the possibilities that the sport offered.

As he stepped onto the hallowed grounds of the major league stadium, Alex carried with him the hopes of every player who ever felt the sting of doubt or the weight of adversity. The crack of his bat echoed not only through the cavernous stadium but through the collective aspirations of those who, like him, harbored dreams of gracing the grand stage of professional baseball.

His debut was more than just a personal accomplishment—it symbolized breaking barriers and defying preconceived notions about who could ascend to the pinnacle of the sport. In that moment, a message resonated beyond the confines of the diamond: that talent recognizes no predetermined boundaries, and the tenacity to pursue one's dreams can surmount any obstacle.

Alex Rodriguez's major league debut was a celebration not only for fans of the game but for anyone who has ever faced adversity and questioned their capacity to achieve greatness. It became a rallying point for those who understood that the journey from a modest background to the grandeur of Major League Baseball was a collective victory, one that inspired generations of young players to persevere in the face of challenges and pursue their own breakthrough moments.

In the annals of baseball history, Alex Rodriguez's Major League debut stands as a beacon of inspiration—a vivid testament to the transformative power of dedication, perseverance, and the unwavering belief that, regardless of origin, every player has the potential to leave an indelible mark on the sport they love.

Reflection and Legacy: A Journey Beyond the Diamond

In moments of introspection, Alex Rodriguez found himself retracing the contours of his extraordinary journey—a voyage that transcended the boundaries of a baseball diamond and left an indelible mark on his character. This chapter unveils the profound impact of mentors, teammates, and the essence of the game, shaping not merely a baseball player but a man of enduring character.

Gratitude to Mentors

In the quiet corridors of reflection, Alex extends gratitude to the mentors who played instrumental roles in his evolution. Seasoned coaches sculpted his technique, and veteran players shared nuanced insights, transforming the baseball diamond into a classroom of life's profound lessons. Their influence extended beyond the mechanics of the sport, imparting wisdom on integrity, sportsmanship, and the responsibilities accompanying success.

Bonds with Teammates

Within the camaraderie of the baseball brotherhood, teammates cease to be mere compatriots on the field. They become companions in the collective pursuit of excellence. Victories and defeats, shared triumphs, and mutual challenges weave a tapestry of collaboration. For Alex, baseball metamorphoses into a symphony where every player contributes to the harmonious pursuit of a common goal.

Life Lessons Beyond the Diamond

As the cheers fade and the stadium lights dim, life lessons gleaned from baseball emerge in Alex's character. The resilience honed in overcoming on-field challenges becomes an indomitable spirit confronting life's adversities. The ethos of teamwork ingrained in dugouts becomes a blueprint for navigating relationships, workplaces, and the broader canvas of life.

Enduring Power of Dreams

The recurring theme in Alex's reflection is the enduring power of dreams. Dreams that propel a young boy from a modest neighborhood to the grand stages of Major League Baseball aren't mere aspirations—they are dynamic forces shaping destinies. In the narrative of his journey, Alex underscores that dreams are not passive fantasies but dynamic catalysts for transformation, propelling endeavors beyond the realm of sports.

A Legacy Defined

Beyond records and accolades, Alex Rodriguez's legacy emerges as a testament to the transformative journey facilitated by baseball. Resilience, teamwork, and belief in the enduring power of dreams become the pillars of a legacy reaching far beyond box scores. It is a legacy that inspires not only aspiring baseball players but anyone striving for personal growth and success.

In these contemplative moments, Alex recognizes that his journey in baseball isn't merely about games played and victories won. It's about lives touched, lessons learned, and an enduring impact on the human spirit. As the final chapters of his playing career unfold, the legacy of Alex Rodriguez extends beyond the diamond, resonating as a beacon for those who dare to dream and persevere—both within the lines of a baseball field and in the broader game of life.

Chapter 3: Teamwork and Friendship: A Tapestry of Bonds

In the grand tapestry of baseball, where every swing of the bat and every catch in the outfield weaves a story, the threads of teamwork and friendship stand out as vibrant hues. Baseball is not merely a game of individual skill; it's a collective effort where the symphony of collaboration echoes through every inning. In this chapter, we unravel tales that showcase the power of teamwork, emphasizing the profound impact of camaraderie on and off the field.

A Unified Infield: The "Turn Two" Magic
In the annals of baseball history, the 1970s witnessed the rise of a dynamic duo that elevated the execution of the double play to an art form. Enter Joe Morgan and Dave Concepción, a formidable pair

whose synergy in the Cincinnati Reds' infield became legendary, epitomizing the essence of teamwork in the sport.

Joe Morgan, a second baseman known for his agility, keen baseball IQ, and offensive prowess, formed an inseparable partnership with shortstop Dave Concepción. Together, they redefined the concept of turning two—transforming routine double plays into a ballet of coordinated movements that left spectators and opponents alike in awe.

Their ability to anticipate each other's actions transcended the mechanics of the game. Morgan's instinctual understanding of Concepción's positioning and vice versa created a seamless defensive ballet. It was not merely a partnership born of practice but a telepathic connection that unfolded in the split seconds between a ground ball and the crack of the bat.

The impact of Morgan and Concepción's collaboration extended far beyond the routine highlight reels. Their adept double-play executions became a cornerstone of the Reds' success during the 1970s, contributing significantly to the team's triumphs, including their World Series victory in 1975.

Their partnership set an enduring standard for infield collaborations, influencing generations of players who aspired to replicate the "Turn Two" magic. Young infielders across the baseball landscape studied the nuances of Morgan and Concepción's seamless coordination, recognizing that their success was rooted not just in individual skill but in the profound artistry of working as a synchronized unit.

As we explore the historical chapters of baseball, the legacy of Joe Morgan and Dave Concepción stands as a testament to the profound impact that teamwork can have on the field. The echoes of their "Turn Two" magic continue to resonate, not only in the pages of baseball lore but also in the strategies employed by infielders seeking to emulate the standard set by this iconic duo.

Pitcher-Catcher Bond: Guiding the Team's Destiny
In the heart of every successful pitching staff lies an unspoken understanding between the pitcher and catcher. One such legendary pair was Greg Maddux and Greg Olson, who played pivotal roles for the Atlanta Braves in the 1990s. Maddux's precision on the mound and Olson's expert guidance created a synergy that went beyond strategy—it was a shared vision that propelled the Braves to a historic era of dominance.

The Outfield Brotherhood: Pursuing Dreams in Vast Expanse
In the realm of baseball, the vast outfield unfolds as a canvas where dreams are pursued, and victories are chased down with meticulous precision. Beyond the confines of the diamond, the outfield stands as a unique domain demanding an extraordinary form of collaboration. Outfielders, guardians of the distant boundaries, embark on a journey where communication becomes the linchpin, and the pursuit of fly balls is a ballet of shared trust.

In the rich tapestry of baseball history, the outfield partnerships of legends like Willie Mays and Monte Irvin stand out as exemplars of seamless collaboration. Their alliance in the New York Giants outfield during the 1950s not only showcased athletic prowess but illuminated the vital role of trust and communication in sculpting an impervious defensive bastion.

The Symphony of Movement: Willie Mays and Monte Irvin
Willie Mays, renowned as the "Say Hey Kid," possessed an otherworldly ability to cover vast expanses of the outfield with grace and speed. His partner in this outfield symphony, Monte Irvin, complemented Mays's brilliance with a blend of experience and baseball acumen. Together, they orchestrated a ballet of coordinated movement, anticipating each other's actions in a silent language born of shared commitment.

Chasing Down Fly Balls: The Precision of Pursuit
Outfielders, bound by a mutual understanding, must navigate the expansive field with a precision akin to dancers on a stage. The pursuit of fly balls becomes a shared endeavor, where split-second decisions and synchronized movements can mean the difference between securing a crucial out and conceding a game-changing hit. Mays and Irvin, in their outfield ballet, epitomized this precision, showcasing an intuitive connection that transformed the outfield into a stage for extraordinary feats.

Creating an Impenetrable Defensive Wall: Trust and Communication
In the outfield, trust is the mortar that binds the bricks of individual talent, forming an impenetrable defensive wall. Mays and Irvin, through their shared experiences and countless hours of practice, cultivated a level of trust that allowed them to roam the vast expanse with a shared purpose. The unspoken communication between them was a testament to the profound connection forged through shared victories and the challenges of the game.

Legacy Beyond the Outfield Fences
The legacy of outfield partnerships extends beyond the boundaries of the game. The stories of Mays and Irvin continue to echo through baseball lore, serving as a beacon for aspiring outfielders. Their collaboration was not merely a defensive strategy; it was a narrative of friendship, mutual respect, and the enduring impact that a united outfield can have on the outcome of a game.

Conclusion: Beyond the Outfield Horizon
As we explore the outfield brotherhood, the tales of Willie Mays and Monte Irvin illuminate a truth that resonates through the ages. In the vastness of the outfield, where dreams soar and victories are chased, collaboration becomes an art form. The outfield is not just a physical expanse; it is a canvas where the bonds of trust and communication paint a portrait of baseball excellence. In the chapters that follow, we delve deeper into the layers of camaraderie and teamwork that define the very essence of the sport.

The Clubhouse Chemistry: Building Championship Teams
In the annals of baseball history, the essence of a championship team extends far beyond the diamond—it permeates the very air within the clubhouse. This truth found vivid expression in the 1980s Oakland Athletics, famously known as the "Bash Brothers." Here, the bonds of camaraderie were not mere embellishments to skill but the bedrock upon which championships were forged.

Jose Canseco and Mark McGwire emerged as the dynamic duo of power hitting, but it was the authentic affection they shared that truly set the Athletics apart. Their connection was more than a strategic alliance;

it was a genuine friendship that created a culture of unity, a culture that became the secret weapon behind multiple championships.

In the hallowed space of the Athletics' clubhouse, camaraderie blossomed into a force of unparalleled strength. The Bash Brothers' power on the field was mirrored by the strength of their friendship off it. Their genuine bond set the tone for the entire team, creating an environment where every player felt connected to a larger purpose—the pursuit of victory as a unified entity.

The echoes of their camaraderie reverberated through every practice session, every pep talk, and every crucial moment on the field. It wasn't just about individual accomplishments; it was about lifting each other up, sharing the burden of expectations, and celebrating victories together. This synergy became the driving force behind the Athletics' dominance during their championship years.

The Bash Brothers era wasn't merely defined by home runs and accolades; it was distinguished by the palpable sense of brotherhood that enveloped the team. The connection between Canseco and McGwire, and by extension the entire roster, illustrated that championship-caliber teams aren't just collections of talented individuals—they are families bound by a common goal and genuine affection for one another.

As the Athletics clinched championships, the world witnessed the tangible impact of clubhouse chemistry. Opponents may have feared the prowess of Canseco and McGwire at the plate, but what truly made the Athletics formidable was the unbreakable bond between teammates. It was a lesson etched in the history of baseball—a lesson that transcends the sport, reminding us that in the pursuit of greatness, the strength of unity often outshines the brilliance of individual stars.

The story of the Bash Brothers serves as a testament to the enduring truth that championships are not solely won through skill and strategy; they are forged in the crucible of genuine camaraderie and shared purpose. It's a narrative that continues to inspire and resonate with fans and players alike, underscoring the timeless importance of building not just a team, but a brotherhood, on the road to championship glory.

The Modern Era: Cross-Cultural Collaboration
In the dynamic tapestry of modern baseball, the composition of teams has evolved into a harmonious blend of diverse talents and cultural backgrounds. The Houston Astros' triumphant journey to the 2017 World Series championship stands as a compelling testament to the profound impact of cross-cultural collaboration within the sport.

The Astros' roster during that historic season reflected a mosaic of talent, with players such as José Altuve, Carlos Correa, and Yuli Gurriel symbolizing the team's cultural diversity. Altuve, hailing from Venezuela, Correa representing Puerto Rico, and Gurriel, a Cuban defector, brought a rich array of experiences and perspectives to the field.

Beyond the individual prowess of each player, it was the seamless integration of these cultural threads that defined the Astros' success. The language of teamwork, unspoken and universal, bridged any linguistic or cultural barriers that might have hindered other teams. Altuve's lightning-quick reflexes, Correa's defensive prowess, and Gurriel's power at the plate became not just individual strengths but interconnected elements of a collective force.

The clubhouse culture of the Astros during the 2017 season exemplified an environment where diversity was celebrated, and unity was paramount. The players' shared commitment to a common goal overshadowed any differences in language or background. Their ability to understand and complement each other's playing styles transformed the Astros into an unstoppable force, culminating in a World Series victory that echoed the team's resilience, adaptability, and collective spirit.

José Altuve's leadership on the field, Carlos Correa's clutch performances, and Yuli Gurriel's infectious enthusiasm were not only integral to the Astros' success but also emblematic of a broader shift in baseball dynamics. The story of the 2017 Astros goes beyond wins and losses; it becomes a narrative of how a team, forged through a mosaic of cultural influences, can redefine the norms of success in the modern era.

As we explore these tales of collaboration, the Houston Astros' 2017 triumph stands as a shining example—a reminder that in the ever-evolving landscape of baseball, the strength of a team lies not only in individual talents but in the collective synergy of players, regardless of their diverse origins. The chapters that follow will continue to unravel the intricacies of human connection and collaboration within the sport, showcasing how the shared pursuit of victory transcends cultural boundaries and creates enduring bonds on the baseball field.

Off the Field: Bonds Beyond Baseball

In the world of baseball, the threads of camaraderie often extend far beyond the confines of the diamond, weaving a narrative that transcends the game itself. One such tale of enduring friendship unfolds between two legendary figures, Derek Jeter and Jorge Posada, whose connection goes beyond the shared victories and defeats witnessed on the field.

Derek Jeter and Jorge Posada: A Bond Beyond Baseball

The New York Yankees, perennial contenders in the American League, witnessed the emergence of a dynamic duo whose friendship became synonymous with the team's success. Derek Jeter, the iconic shortstop, and Jorge Posada, the steadfast catcher, formed a bond that surpassed the boundaries of professional collaboration.

Shared Triumphs and Defeats

Jeter and Posada's journey together began in the minor leagues, where their shared dreams of donning the iconic pinstripes of the Yankees took root. As they ascended to the grand stage of Yankee Stadium, their partnership evolved into more than just a battery of shortstop and catcher—it became a pillar of stability amid the uncertainties of the game.

The late 1990s and early 2000s saw the Yankees capture multiple World Series titles, with Jeter and Posada at the forefront of these championship runs. Their on-field synchronicity was palpable, with Jeter's acrobatic plays at shortstop complemented by Posada's strategic prowess behind the plate. Beyond the box scores, their camaraderie became a driving force in the Yankees' pursuit of excellence.

Shared Values Beyond the Game

Off the field, the friendship between Jeter and Posada deepened. Their shared experiences forged a connection grounded in mutual respect, trust, and a commitment to excellence that extended beyond the realm of baseball. Whether navigating the pressures of the postseason or supporting each other during personal challenges, their friendship became a source of strength.

Life Beyond Baseball

As their playing careers advanced, Jeter and Posada's bond continued to flourish. Their off-season endeavors and philanthropic efforts showcased a shared commitment to making a positive impact beyond the game. Together, they embraced roles as leaders and mentors, leaving an indelible mark on the Yankees' legacy and inspiring a new generation of players.

Legacy of Friendship

In 2014, Jeter bid farewell to the game he had graced for two decades. The enduring image of his final game at Yankee Stadium, with Posada among those paying tribute, encapsulated the depth of their connection. Beyond the scripted narratives of sports, their enduring friendship became a testament to the profound impact of camaraderie on personal and professional growth.

Conclusion: The Ripple Effect

Derek Jeter and Jorge Posada's friendship stands as a testament to the enduring bonds forged through the crucible of baseball. Their story resonates not only as a chapter in the history of the New York Yankees but as a broader narrative of friendship's ability to shape lives. As we move forward in our exploration of baseball's inspirational stories, the ripple effect of such enduring connections will continue to underscore the profound impact of human connections within the world of sports.

Conclusion: The Enduring Tapestry of Teamwork and Friendship

As we journey through the rich tapestry of baseball's history, the indomitable spirit of teamwork and friendship stands as an everlasting testament to the essence of the sport. These stories, drawn from decades past to the present era, form the threads that weave together a vibrant narrative of bonds forged on the diamond. Teamwork transcends being a mere strategy; it is the pulsating heartbeat of baseball—a rhythmic resonance that echoes through every crack of the bat, every spectacular play, and every shared triumph.

In the annals of baseball lore, the exploits of legendary pairs such as Joe Morgan and Dave Concepción, whose balletic prowess turned double plays into an art form, showcase the profound impact of collaboration. Their synchronicity wasn't just a display of skill; it was a manifestation of the unspoken understanding that elevates a team to greatness.

The pitcher-catcher duos, like Greg Maddux and Greg Olson, remind us that success on the mound is not a solitary achievement. It is a collaborative effort where trust and synergy between battery mates guide the destiny of the entire team.

Venturing into the outfield, the tales of partnerships like Willie Mays and Monte Irvin underscore the importance of communication and coordination in tracking down dreams—fly balls that seem destined for the gaps but fall harmlessly into a waiting glove, a testament to the outfielders' unspoken agreement.

Championship teams, from the "Bash Brothers" era of the Oakland Athletics to the cross-cultural collaboration of the Houston Astros, illuminate the significance of clubhouse chemistry. Their shared triumphs were not just a result of individual brilliance; they were the culmination of friendships that extended beyond the field, creating an unbreakable bond that fueled their collective success.

As we conclude this exploration of teamwork and friendship, we recognize that these themes are not confined to the diamond. The enduring friendship between Derek Jeter and Jorge Posada stands as a real-world testament to the profound impact of camaraderie. Their bond, nurtured through years of shared victories and defeats, exemplifies how the relationships formed on the baseball field can extend far beyond, shaping lives and becoming enduring lessons for all.

In the chapters that follow, we will delve deeper into the human spirit intertwined with the game—the resilience that defines comebacks, the transformative power of breakthroughs, and the timeless moments that transcend baseball to become lessons that resonate not just within the confines of the diamond but in the tapestry of life itself.

Chapter 4: The Comeback Kid: Stories of Resilience

In the tumultuous world of baseball, where triumphs and setbacks often dance in tandem, the stories of those who faced adversity head-on and emerged victorious are the stuff of legend. This chapter delves into the tales of players who earned the moniker of "The Comeback Kid," players whose indomitable spirits and resilience in the face of setbacks have become a source of inspiration for generations.

Introduction: Navigating Life's Curveballs

In the vast arena of baseball, a microcosm of life's uncertainties unfolds—a narrative woven with unexpected twists and turns. This chapter is a testament to the resilience inherent in the sport, showcasing players who embody the profound capacity to metamorphose setbacks into resounding comebacks. These athletes, whose journeys are etched in the annals of the game, have faced challenges transcending the confines of physical prowess, delving deep into the terrain of mental fortitude. Their stories illuminate the essence of baseball, a realm where determination and grit extend far beyond the manicured fields to resonate with the human spirit's indomitable will to rise from adversity.

The Broken Streak: Derek Jeter's Resurgence

In the storied career of Derek Jeter, the legendary shortstop for the New York Yankees, a critical juncture unfolded that would test the mettle of the Captain and redefine his place in baseball history. The stage was the playoffs, the stakes were high, and an unforeseen injury threatened to eclipse the brilliance of an illustrious career.

During a pivotal postseason game, Jeter suffered a significant setback—a broken ankle. The injury cast a shadow of uncertainty over the future of a player whose name had become synonymous with excellence. Doubts surfaced, not only about the continuation of his career but also about whether he could reclaim the field at the same extraordinary level that had defined him.

In the face of this adversity, Jeter's commitment to the game became a beacon of resilience. His response was not defined by despair but fueled by an unwavering work ethic that had been a hallmark of his career. The rehabilitation journey that followed was not merely a physical one; it became a testament to the mental fortitude that set Jeter apart as a true leader.

The grueling rehabilitation process, marked by tireless hours of physical therapy, strength conditioning, and the relentless pursuit of recovery, revealed the essence of Jeter's character. His determination to return to the field, not as a shadow of his former self but as the embodiment of his legendary status, was unwavering.

The Captain's comeback was not just about stepping back onto the diamond; it was a resurrection of grace, leadership, and skill. The qualities that had defined him throughout his career were not compromised by the injury; instead, they were accentuated. Jeter's return was a narrative of triumph, a living testament to the idea that setbacks are not endpoints but rather integral chapters in the longer story of resilience.

As he reclaimed his position, Jeter did not merely resume playing; he continued to lead with the same poise that had earned him the title of Captain. His impact extended beyond statistics and victories; it was a reaffirmation that setbacks, no matter how daunting, could be overcome through sheer determination and an unyielding love for the game.

Derek Jeter's resurgence serves as an inspiration not just for baseball enthusiasts but for anyone navigating challenges in life. His story transcends the boundaries of the field, offering a compelling reminder that the true measure of a person is not in avoiding setbacks but in the manner of their return. In the saga of Derek Jeter, the broken streak was not the end; it was a pivotal chapter that underscored the resilience of a baseball icon.

Overcoming Adversity: Josh Hamilton's Resilient Journey
In the unforgiving landscape of professional baseball, few stories mirror the challenges faced by outfielder Josh Hamilton. His career, marked by extraordinary talent, took a tumultuous turn due to personal struggles and addiction, threatening to permanently sideline one of the

sport's most promising stars. Yet, Hamilton's journey stands as a testament to resilience, redemption, and the enduring power of the human spirit.

The Descent and the Battle Within

Josh Hamilton's ascent to the major leagues was nothing short of meteoric, earning him accolades and establishing him as a force to be reckoned with on the field. However, his trajectory took an unexpected and harrowing turn when personal demons, in the form of addiction, cast a shadow over his promising career. The battle within became as formidable as any opponent he faced on the diamond, leading to a hiatus that left fans and teammates uncertain about his future.

The Abyss and the Road to Redemption

During this dark period, Hamilton's career seemed at the brink of collapse. His struggles with addiction led to suspensions and an uncertain future. However, his story takes a transformative turn when he found unwavering support from those who believed in his redemption, including his family, teammates, and the Texas Rangers organization. It was this support system that became the cornerstone of his journey back to the sport he loved.

A Return to the Diamond: Triumph Over Inner Struggles

Hamilton's return to the baseball diamond was more than a physical comeback; it was a triumph over profound inner struggles. The arduous path to recovery, marked by rehabilitation and personal reflection, showcased not only his dedication to the game but also his commitment to conquering the demons that had threatened to derail his career. It became a story of personal redemption and the resilience required to emerge stronger from the depths of adversity.

A Beacon of Hope

As Josh Hamilton stepped back onto the field, his journey became a beacon of hope for those facing similar battles, both within and outside the realm of baseball. His resilience demonstrated that the path to redemption is paved with challenges, but with determination, a robust support system, and an unyielding will to confront personal demons, triumph is not only achievable but transformative.

Legacy of Resilience

Hamilton's story extends beyond the box scores and highlights. It is a living testament to the complexities of the human experience, the impact of addiction, and the triumph that arises from confronting and overcoming personal struggles. His legacy serves as a source of inspiration for individuals grappling with adversity, reminding them that, even in the darkest moments, the possibility of redemption and resurgence exists.

In recounting the chapters of Josh Hamilton's life, we witness not only a return to the sport but the emergence of a stronger, more resilient individual. His journey underscores the profound truth that, in the arena of professional sports and life alike, triumph over inner struggles is a victory that transcends the game itself.

From Surgery to Stardom: Tommy John's Pioneering Resilience

In the rich tapestry of baseball history, few tales rival the saga of Tommy John, a pitcher whose very name has become synonymous with a groundbreaking surgical procedure. Yet, behind the medical moniker lies a narrative of unwavering determination, resilience, and a remarkable journey from a career-threatening elbow injury to a lasting legacy that transcends the boundaries of the sport.

A Pitcher's Peril

Tommy John, an accomplished pitcher with a storied career, found himself at a crossroads when a debilitating elbow injury jeopardized his future in the game. The severity of the injury raised doubts about the possibility of a return to the pitcher's mound. This was not merely a physical setback; it was a challenge to the core of his identity as an athlete.

The Surgical Solution

Undeterred by the grim prognosis, Tommy John embraced a revolutionary surgical solution proposed by Dr. Frank Jobe. In 1974, John became the first Major League Baseball player to undergo ulnar collateral ligament (UCL) reconstruction, now widely known as "Tommy John surgery." The procedure involved replacing the damaged ligament in his pitching elbow with a tendon from his forearm, a medical innovation that would redefine the trajectory of baseball careers.

A Pioneering Comeback

The surgical intervention was not just a shot at redemption for Tommy John; it was a pioneering journey into uncharted territory. The extensive rehabilitation process and the uncertainties surrounding the success of the surgery did little to deter his resolve. John approached his recovery with the same discipline and dedication that marked his pitching career.

Triumph Over Adversity

The 1976 season marked Tommy John's triumphant return to the pitcher's mound, just over a year after undergoing the groundbreaking surgery. His comeback was not just a personal victory; it was a beacon of hope for athletes grappling with career-threatening injuries. John's resilience and success after surgery demonstrated that setbacks could be surmounted through a combination of medical innovation and an athlete's indomitable spirit.

Revolutionizing the Game

Tommy John's return to stardom after UCL reconstruction surgery sent ripples through the baseball community. The procedure, initially met with skepticism, gained acceptance and became a standard practice for pitchers facing similar injuries. What began as a personal quest for revival had morphed into a transformative moment in the history of sports medicine, forever changing how athletes approached and overcame elbow injuries.

Enduring Legacy

The legacy of Tommy John extends far beyond his impressive statistics or accolades. His journey from surgery to stardom left an indelible mark on the sport, inspiring countless athletes to navigate the challenges of injury with hope and determination. The term "Tommy John surgery" became more than a medical procedure; it became a symbol of resilience, a testament to the idea that setbacks could be the catalyst for groundbreaking comebacks.

Conclusion

Tommy John's enduring legacy stands as a testament to the intersection of medical innovation and athletic perseverance. His journey from the brink of a career-ending injury to a pioneering comeback reshaped not only his own narrative but also the landscape of baseball. As players continue to undergo "Tommy John surgery" and reclaim their positions on the field, they owe a debt of gratitude to a pitcher who, in the face of adversity, elevated a personal setback into a triumph that reverberates through the corridors of baseball history.

The Resilience of "The Say Hey Kid": Willie Mays' Remarkable Comeback

In the annals of baseball history, few names evoke the same reverence as Willie Mays, affectionately known as "The Say Hey Kid." Yet, even legends like Mays faced the inevitabilities of aging and the toll it took on his once-dominant performance.

As Mays ventured deeper into the latter stages of his illustrious career, the signs of wear and tear became more apparent. The speed that defined his early years, the agility that made him an outfield maestro, and the power that characterized his swing all showed signs of decline. The baseball world witnessed a temporary dip in the trajectory of a player whose name was synonymous with greatness.

However, it was during this challenging phase that Willie Mays demonstrated a resolve that transcended the statistics on a scorecard. His commitment to the craft, honed over decades, became the driving force behind a late-career resurgence that captivated fans and solidified his legacy as one of the game's enduring figures.

Amid whispers of doubt and skepticism, Mays, fueled by an unwavering love for the game, embarked on a journey of adaptation and reinvention. While the physical attributes of his youth may have waned, Mays compensated with an astute understanding of the game, a veteran's wisdom, and an unparalleled work ethic.

The outfield became not just a field of play for Mays, but a canvas upon which he painted a narrative of resilience. Despite the inevitable passage of time, Mays displayed an intuitive sense of the game's nuances, positioning himself with strategic mastery and reading plays with the acumen of a seasoned maestro.

It wasn't merely about defying age; it was about embracing the evolving dynamics of the sport. Mays' late-career heroics were not measured solely in home runs and stolen bases but in the subtle yet impactful moments that defined a seasoned player's contribution.

As he navigated the latter chapters of his playing days, Willie Mays showed that passion, dedication, and a profound love for the game could transcend the limitations imposed by a birth certificate. His resurgence was not an isolated feat but rather a testament to the enduring spirit that fuels the heart of a true athlete.

For fans, witnessing "The Say Hey Kid" back in form was not just a nostalgic journey but a living testament to the timelessness of greatness. In every swing, every catch, and every stolen base, Mays etched another chapter in his storied career, leaving an indelible mark on the sport he had graced for so long.

Willie Mays' comeback wasn't merely a statistical rebound; it was a narrative of triumph over the inevitable, a living embodiment of the enduring spirit that defines a baseball legend. Through his journey, young readers can glean not only the technical aspects of the game but also the intangible qualities that separate the great from the legendary. Age, as Mays demonstrated, is indeed just a number when coupled with an unwavering passion for the game.

Rising from Adversity: Josh Beckett's Inspiring Redemption

In the unpredictable realm of professional baseball, the narrative of Josh Beckett stands as a testament to the resilience that defines the sport's true champions. Known for his fierce competitiveness and a storied career, Beckett encountered a formidable low marked by a combination of injuries and performance struggles that left pundits questioning the longevity of his journey on the mound.

As injuries took their toll and doubts circulated within the baseball community, Beckett found himself at a crossroads that could have signaled the premature end of an illustrious career. However, instead of succumbing to the prevailing narrative of decline, he chose to author his own story of redemption.

Embracing a journey fraught with uncertainty, Beckett exemplified unwavering resilience, channeling his trademark determination into a meticulous regimen of recovery and rehabilitation. The pitcher's mound, once a site of triumphs, became a testing ground for his mettle and an arena where doubts transformed into fuel for his resurgence.

Hard work became Beckett's ally, as he engaged in a relentless pursuit to reclaim the form that had made him a formidable force on the field. Hours of rehabilitation, conditioning, and a commitment to his craft defined the arduous path he undertook. Beyond the physical challenges, Beckett faced the mental rigors that accompany the quest for redemption — a journey marked not only by external doubts but also the internal dialogue of a competitor unwilling to concede defeat.

The turning point came not in a single triumphant moment but through a gradual process of reinvention. Beckett's return to the mound wasn't merely a resumption of duty; it was a statement, a proclamation that setbacks are but interludes in the grand narrative of a baseball career.

What emerged from this narrative of redemption was a pitcher transformed. Beckett not only regained his physical prowess but also exhibited a newfound maturity and strategic acumen that spoke to the depth of his commitment to the game. His triumphant return was not just a testament to overcoming physical adversity but an embodiment of the indomitable spirit that defines a true athlete.

Aspiring players and seasoned veterans alike found inspiration in Josh Beckett's journey. His story serves as a beacon of hope for those navigating their own challenges, emphasizing that setbacks, though formidable, are not insurmountable barriers. Josh Beckett's redemption was not merely a personal victory; it was a reaffirmation of the enduring spirit that propels athletes to rise from adversity, reshaping their narratives and etching their names in the annals of baseball history.

Conclusion: Embracing Resilience Beyond the Diamond
As we reflect on the compelling journeys of these comeback athletes, their narratives extend far beyond the confines of the baseball diamond, transcending the realm of sports to become universal stories of resilience, courage, and triumph.

In the unpredictable game of life, setbacks, be they physical injuries or personal struggles, are not the final chapters of our stories. Instead, they represent pivotal junctures—a call to resilience, an invitation to reinvent oneself, and ultimately, an opportunity for triumphant comebacks.

These players faced adversity head-on, confronting challenges that would have daunted many. Yet, their return to the game was not merely a reentry; it was a resurgence marked by a renewed vigor that elevated them to the status of true legends. Their ability to transform setbacks into stepping stones and emerge stronger on the other side immortalizes them not just as athletes but as beacons of inspiration for anyone navigating the unpredictable terrain of life.

As young readers embark on their own journeys, facing trials and tribulations, they can draw profound inspiration from these tales. The stories within these pages are not isolated incidents but guideposts, illuminating the path forward. Setbacks are not impassable roadblocks but rather opportunities for growth, development, and the forging of character.

The essence of a true comeback lies not solely in overcoming obstacles but in the metamorphosis that occurs during the process. It is about emerging from challenges stronger, wiser, and more determined than ever before. These athletes exemplify that the true measure of success lies not only in the victories on the field but in the resilience displayed when faced with adversity.

So, as we bid farewell to the pages of this chapter, let us carry with us the invaluable lessons of resilience, the spirit of reinvention, and the understanding that triumph is not a destination but a continuous journey. May the stories of these comeback kids echo in the hearts of young readers, encouraging them to face challenges with unwavering determination, knowing that they possess the innate strength to transform setbacks into their own triumphant comebacks.

Chapter 5: Beyond the Game: Players Making a Difference

In the grand tapestry of baseball, certain players transcend the boundaries of the field, becoming catalysts for positive change in society. This chapter delves into the stories of athletes whose impact extends far beyond the diamond, showcasing how their commitment to social causes has left an enduring legacy.

Roberto Clemente: The Humanitarian Hero

In the storied history of baseball, the name Roberto Clemente stands as a beacon not only for his remarkable prowess as a right fielder but equally for his steadfast dedication to humanitarian causes. Hailing from the vibrant island of Puerto Rico, Clemente elevated his role as an athlete to that of a passionate advocate for social justice and equality.

Roberto Clemente's impact extended far beyond the confines of the baseball field. His commitment to philanthropy was not a mere footnote in his storied career but rather a defining aspect of his legacy. Born on August 18, 1934, in Carolina, Puerto Rico, Clemente's early life was shaped by the richness of his cultural heritage and the challenges of a world still grappling with racial and social disparities.

From the onset of his professional career with the Pittsburgh Pirates in 1955, Clemente used his burgeoning platform to champion causes close to his heart. His notable contributions ranged from organizing impactful charity initiatives to personally delivering aid to disaster-stricken regions, leaving an indelible mark on the lives of those he touched.

Clemente's humanitarian efforts were particularly pronounced during times of crisis. In 1972, following a devastating earthquake in Nicaragua, he organized and personally oversaw the delivery of supplies and aid to the affected communities. Tragically, just months later, on December 31, 1972, Clemente's life was cut short when the plane carrying relief supplies he had personally organized crashed off the coast of Puerto Rico.

His legacy, however, endures as a poignant reminder that athletes wield a unique power to effect change beyond the realms of their respective sports. Clemente's dedication to bettering the lives of those in need transcends generations, and the impact of his charitable work is felt not only in the communities he directly served but also in the collective consciousness of those who continue to draw inspiration from his selfless commitment to humanitarian causes.

In 1973, Clemente was posthumously awarded the Presidential Medal of Freedom, an honor reflecting the magnitude of his contributions both on and off the baseball diamond. The Roberto Clemente Award, established in 1971 to honor the player who best exemplifies sportsmanship, community involvement, and contribution to his team, further cements his status as a humanitarian hero in the world of sports.

Roberto Clemente's enduring legacy serves as a testament to the transformative power of using one's platform for social good. As young readers delve into his story, they are not only witnesses to the feats of a baseball legend but also participants in a narrative that underscores the profound impact athletes can have when they choose to stand for something larger than the game.

Jackie Robinson: A Champion for Equality Beyond the Bases
The name Jackie Robinson is eternally intertwined with the historic moment he stepped onto a major league baseball field, breaking the color barrier in 1947. His impact, however, transcends the confines of the diamond, revealing a man whose commitment to equality and justice resonated far beyond the realm of sports.

Off the field, Robinson evolved into a resolute advocate for the civil rights movement, his efforts reaching beyond the stadium lights. His advocacy was not merely symbolic; it was a manifestation of his unwavering dedication to combating racial inequality. Robinson's tireless work included active involvement in various charitable organizations dedicated to addressing the socio-economic disparities faced by African Americans.

Beyond the glamour of the baseball world, Robinson's unyielding dedication was felt in boardrooms, courtrooms, and classrooms alike. Recognizing the power of education as a vehicle for societal change, he championed initiatives that aimed to level the playing field for African Americans. Scholarships, mentorship programs, and support for educational institutions became key components of his mission to foster equal opportunities for all.

Robinson's legacy stands as a testament to the enduring power of courage and activism. He confronted prejudice with grace, shouldering the responsibility of being a trailblazer with resilience and poise. His journey from the baseball field to the forefront of the civil rights movement exemplifies the profound impact one individual can have in reshaping societal norms.

As the echoes of Robinson's legacy reverberate through history, his life serves as a compelling lesson in the potency of principled action. Young readers are invited to delve into the story of a man who, armed with a baseball bat and an unyielding spirit, paved the way for a more inclusive and just society. Jackie Robinson's legacy is not just a chapter in baseball history; it is an enduring testament to the capacity of sports to drive social change.

Curtis Granderson: A Beacon for Education and Empowerment

In the realm of baseball luminaries, Curtis Granderson stands out not only for his exceptional skills patrolling center field but also for the profound impact he has made in the realm of education. Granderson's journey from the outfield to the forefront of educational advocacy demonstrates the transformative power an athlete can wield beyond the confines of the baseball diamond.

Recognizing the potential of education to shape lives, Granderson founded the Grand Kids Foundation, a testament to his commitment to empowering children through learning. This foundation stands as a testament to Granderson's belief that access to quality education is a key driver for individual and societal progress.

The Grand Kids Foundation strategically channels its efforts through various educational initiatives, each designed to create a ripple effect of positive change. Scholarship programs, a cornerstone of the foundation's work, provide tangible support to aspiring students, unlocking doors to academic opportunities that might have otherwise remained closed. By investing in the educational pursuits of young minds, Granderson extends a helping hand to those who harbor dreams beyond the ballpark.

Book donations form another integral aspect of Granderson's philanthropic endeavors. By putting books into the hands of children, he seeks to ignite the flame of curiosity and a love for learning. These contributions not only bridge educational gaps but also cultivate a culture of literacy that can transcend generations.

Beyond scholarships and book donations, Granderson's foundation dedicates resources to supporting educational infrastructure. By investing in the physical spaces where learning takes place, Granderson ensures that the environment is conducive to growth and development. This commitment speaks to the comprehensive approach he takes to uplift educational systems and create lasting impact.

Granderson's advocacy for education underscores the notion that baseball players can be formidable advocates for a brighter future. His efforts extend far beyond the field, resonating in classrooms, libraries, and communities touched by the transformative power of education. As a champion for knowledge and opportunity, Curtis Granderson embodies the idea that success in baseball need not be confined to the scoreboard; it can be measured in the lives positively influenced and the doors of possibility swung wide open for generations to come.

Adam Jones: A Champion Against Racism
In the realm of baseball, Adam Jones stands not only as a formidable force in the outfield but also as a resolute ambassador against racism. His journey extends beyond the meticulously manicured fields, as Jones has positioned himself as a prominent voice both within and outside the realms of America's pastime.

Known for his stellar defensive prowess, Jones has not merely relied on his athletic skills to define his legacy. In the face of racial injustice, he has stepped into the arena of activism, becoming a vocal advocate for inclusivity and diversity. His commitment extends far beyond performative gestures, manifesting in tangible actions aimed at combating systemic racism.

Jones's impact is palpable in his financial contributions to initiatives dedicated to dismantling racial barriers. Through strategic investments and philanthropy, he has supported organizations at the forefront of the fight against discrimination. His monetary commitments signal not only a personal dedication but also a recognition of the broader responsibility that comes with his influence.

Beyond financial support, Jones has actively engaged in mentorship programs designed to uplift and empower the next generation. His involvement goes beyond symbolic gestures, as he invests time and personal commitment to guide and inspire young individuals. By fostering mentorship programs, Jones recognizes the transformative potential of personal connections and mentor-mentee relationships in dismantling the barriers that perpetuate racial inequality.

In his role as an ambassador against racism, Jones leverages his platform to advocate for enduring change. Through public speaking engagements, interviews, and social media, he ensures that his voice resounds in conversations about racial justice. By confronting systemic issues head-on, Jones exemplifies the idea that athletes are not just performers on the field; they are catalysts for societal transformation.

As young readers explore Adam Jones's journey, they witness a profound example of an athlete who recognizes the gravity of his influence and actively strives to use it for the betterment of society. His story challenges preconceptions about the role of sports figures, urging a reconsideration of their responsibilities in fostering a more equitable and inclusive world. Adam Jones, both on and off the field, is a testament to the enduring power of an individual to effect meaningful change and, in doing so, leaves an indelible mark on the evolving narrative of baseball and social justice.

Beyond the Game: Players Making a Difference
In the vast landscape of baseball, there exist individuals whose impact transcends the boundaries of the playing field, leaving an enduring legacy of positive change. Among these influential figures stands Clayton Kershaw, a luminary not only for his prowess on the pitcher's mound but equally for his unwavering commitment to philanthropy.

Clayton Kershaw's journey extends beyond the confines of baseball statistics, woven intricately with a dedication to making a meaningful difference in the lives of others. At the heart of this commitment lies the Kershaw's Challenge foundation, a philanthropic venture co-founded by Clayton and his wife, Ellen.

Established in 2011, Kershaw's Challenge has emerged as a beacon of hope, channeling the couple's resources and influence to address pressing societal issues. Education and healthcare are focal points of their philanthropic endeavors, reflecting a deep-seated belief in the transformative power of these fundamental pillars.

Within local communities, Kershaw's impact is tangible and far-reaching. The foundation's initiatives include the creation and support of educational programs designed to empower and uplift underserved youth. From scholarships that open doors to higher education to mentorship programs that provide guidance and support, Kershaw's Challenge manifests its commitment to cultivating a brighter future.

Yet, the ripple effect of Kershaw's philanthropy extends well beyond the borders of his hometown. His influence is felt on an international scale, where the foundation engages in initiatives aimed at improving healthcare accessibility and outcomes in regions facing adversity. By leveraging their platform, Clayton and Ellen Kershaw have become advocates for positive change on a global scale.

The impact of Kershaw's Challenge is not merely measured in financial contributions but in the tangible improvements witnessed in the lives of countless individuals. The couple's hands-on involvement, coupled with a genuine passion for making a difference, resonates with the very essence of baseball—a sport that unites communities and inspires collective action.

As young readers explore Clayton Kershaw's story, they are invited to contemplate the profound influence that athletes can wield beyond the sports arena. Kershaw's journey serves as a testament to the idea that success is not defined solely by on-field achievements but by the positive, lasting change one can instigate in the world. It is a reminder that, much like a perfectly executed pitch, the impact of a compassionate and committed athlete can reach far beyond what the eye can see, leaving an indelible mark on the lives they touch.

Conclusion: A Lasting Legacy of Social Impact

As we reflect on the narratives of these remarkable athletes, it becomes evident that their influence extends beyond the realm of sports. Beyond their prowess on the field, baseball players emerge as influential figures and ambassadors for positive change. This chapter has unveiled stories of players who not only excelled in their athletic pursuits but also made profound contributions to society, leaving an indelible mark on the world.

The tales of Roberto Clemente, Jackie Robinson, Curtis Granderson, Adam Jones, and Clayton Kershaw serve as a testament to the idea that athletes possess the potential to be catalysts for social change. These players utilized their platform and resources to address societal challenges, demonstrating a commitment to making a tangible difference beyond the boundaries of the baseball diamond.

The impact of these athletes exemplifies the broader potential of sports as a vehicle for social change. Through their actions and initiatives, they have illuminated the path for young readers, encouraging them to envision a future where their own endeavors, both within and beyond their chosen field, contribute meaningfully to the well-being of society.

As young readers immerse themselves in these narratives, they are not merely spectators but active participants in a broader conversation about the role of athletes in shaping the world. The stories of these players serve as inspiration, prompting reflection on the multifaceted nature of success. Beyond the final score of a game, success is measured by the positive impact one can have on the lives of others.

In essence, baseball becomes more than a game—it transforms into a platform for social responsibility and positive change. The values cultivated on the field, such as teamwork, perseverance, and inclusivity, extend beyond the diamond and into the fabric of society. The young minds exploring these stories are invited to recognize the immense potential within themselves to effect change, just as their athletic heroes have done.

Baseball, with its rich history and cultural significance, stands as a microcosm of the broader world. It is a realm where athletes not only chase victory but also strive to create a more inclusive and equitable world. These narratives beckon young readers to step onto this field of possibility, armed with the understanding that their actions, both big and small, can contribute to a legacy of positive transformation—a legacy that mirrors the values etched in the hearts of those who play and those who watch with hopeful eyes. The enduring impact of these stories extends an invitation to a future where sports, and the athletes who embody its spirit, play an instrumental role in shaping a world that transcends the boundaries of the playing field.

Chapter 6: Breaking Barriers: Pioneers in the Game

In the storied history of baseball, certain players have transcended the boundaries of the game itself, becoming pioneers who shattered racial, gender, and cultural barriers. These courageous individuals not only left an indelible mark on the sport but also paved the way for a more inclusive and diverse future.

Jackie Robinson: Pioneer of Racial Integration in Baseball

The saga of breaking barriers in the world of baseball commences with the iconic figure of Jackie Robinson, a name inseparable from courage and tenacity. In the pivotal year of 1947, Robinson etched his name into the annals of Major League Baseball, emerging as the first African American to grace the field in the esteemed uniform of the Brooklyn Dodgers. His narrative extends beyond the realm of mere athleticism; it stands as a monumental shift in the racial landscape of the sport.

Jackie Robinson's historic journey was not just a personal odyssey; it was a profound transformation that rippled through the very fabric of the game. The stoic resilience he displayed in the face of virulent discrimination and racial prejudice went beyond the confines of the baseball diamond. It was a beacon of hope, a clarion call for justice that reverberated far beyond the bleachers.

In 1947, as Robinson stepped onto Ebbets Field, he carried the weight of expectations and the hopes of an entire community on his shoulders. Enduring racial slurs, hostility from opposing players, and even threats to his life, Robinson navigated a hostile terrain with unwavering determination. His on-field prowess, characterized by speed, skill, and an indomitable spirit, served as a powerful retort to the discriminatory forces that sought to undermine his place in the game.

Yet, Robinson's impact transcended the statistics on the scorecard. By breaking the color barrier, he opened doors that had long been closed to Black players. His success paved the way for a generation of African American athletes who aspired to follow in his footsteps, transforming the landscape of baseball into a more inclusive and diverse arena.

The enduring legacy of Jackie Robinson extends beyond the confines of the baseball field. His actions ignited a flame that would fuel the broader civil rights movement. His stoic refusal to bow to prejudice became a symbol of resistance and resilience, contributing significantly to the dismantling of racial segregation not only in sports but in society at large.

The fight against racial inequality in America found an unlikely hero in a baseball uniform. Robinson's journey, fraught with challenges and victories alike, remains a testament to the transformative power of sports in fostering societal change. The echoes of his courage persist in every Black player who takes the field, in every fan who celebrates diversity, and in the continued pursuit of equality within the cherished realms of America's favorite pastime. Jackie Robinson's legacy endures, not just as a baseball legend, but as a trailblazer who paved the way for a more just and inclusive future.

Roberto Clemente: Breaking Barriers and Building Bridges
In the tapestry of baseball history, Roberto Clemente emerges as a pivotal figure, transcending not only racial divisions but also bridging the cultural gaps that marked the sport. Hailing from the vibrant landscapes of Puerto Rico, Clemente embarked on a journey that would redefine the expectations for Latin American players in Major League Baseball.

Roberto Clemente's ascent through the ranks of professional baseball was not a mere conquest of pitches and hits; it was a navigation through language barriers and cultural disparities. Puerto Rico, although a U.S. territory, held a distinct cultural identity, and as Clemente made his way to the Major Leagues, he faced the challenge of acclimating not just to a new language but to an entirely different cultural milieu.

Undaunted by these hurdles, Clemente's talent spoke louder than any linguistic or cultural divide. In 1972, he etched his name in the annals of baseball history, becoming the first Latin American player to achieve the milestone of 3,000 hits. This was not merely a statistical triumph; it was a testament to his skill, dedication, and the undeniable charisma that captivated fans across borders.

Clemente's impact, however, stretched far beyond the diamond. Recognizing the platform that his success afforded him, he assumed the role of a humanitarian, using his influence to address pressing social issues. In an era marked by civil rights struggles and social upheaval, Clemente stood as a beacon of change, advocating for justice and equality.

His humanitarian efforts reached their zenith when he spearheaded relief missions to Nicaragua after a devastating earthquake in 1972. Tragically, it was during one such mission that Clemente lost his life in a plane crash on New Year's Eve. The loss of this baseball icon reverberated not only through the sports world but through the realms of humanitarianism and social justice.

Clemente's legacy extends far beyond the statistics and accolades. His life serves as an inspiration, not just for aspiring ballplayers but for anyone seeking to make a positive impact. The Roberto Clemente Award, established in his honor, stands as an annual testament to the player who not only conquered the world of baseball but used his influence to build bridges and pave the way for future generations of Latin American players. In the tapestry of baseball's history, Roberto Clemente remains a trailblazer, his story an enduring testament to the transformative power of talent, charisma, and a commitment to making the world a better place.

Mo'ne Davis: Paving the Way for Women in Baseball

In a pivotal moment for gender equality in baseball, Mo'ne Davis rose to prominence as a trailblazer, challenging stereotypes and redefining what was possible for young girls in the sport. The year 2014 marked a historic chapter in her journey, and at the tender age of 13, Davis captivated the nation's attention with an extraordinary feat at the Little League World Series.

Mo'ne Davis etched her name in the annals of baseball history by becoming the first girl ever to pitch a shutout in the Little League World Series. This achievement wasn't just a statistical triumph; it was a seismic shift in perceptions about the capabilities of female athletes in a traditionally male-dominated sport.

Her prowess on the mound, marked by precision, skill, and an undeniable passion for the game, became a symbol of breaking down gender barriers. Mo'ne Davis wasn't just a player; she was a beacon of inspiration for a new generation of young girls who aspired to step onto the diamond and compete at the highest levels of the sport.

The impact of Mo'ne Davis went beyond her remarkable athletic abilities. She became a symbol of resilience and determination, embodying the idea that skill knows no gender. Her journey ignited a collective realization that talent is indeed universal, irrespective of gender norms that had previously confined the aspirations of young female athletes.

In the wake of Mo'ne Davis's historic performance, a surge of interest and participation among young girls in baseball ensued. Her story became a catalyst for change, encouraging communities to invest in the dreams of aspiring female players. The narrative of Mo'ne Davis transformed from a personal triumph to a communal celebration of progress and inclusivity.

Mo'ne's impact didn't fade with the echoes of her final pitch in the Little League World Series. Instead, her legacy continued to resonate, prompting conversations about equity in sports and the importance of providing equal opportunities for young athletes, regardless of their gender.

As we delve into Mo'ne Davis's story, we find not just a trailblazer on the baseball diamond but a catalyst for a cultural shift in the way we perceive and embrace women in sports. Her journey stands as a testament to the idea that the diamond is a space where talent speaks louder than societal expectations, and every young girl with a love for the game has the right to pursue her passion, unencumbered by limitations based on gender. Mo'ne Davis's legacy endures as an inspiration, inviting future generations to step up to the plate and continue the journey she pioneered—a journey that transcends gender and propels the game of baseball into a more inclusive and diverse future.

Ichiro Suzuki: A Cultural Bridge in the World of Baseball
In the annals of baseball history, few players have achieved the level of cross-cultural impact as Ichiro Suzuki. His journey from Japan to Major League Baseball not only shattered doubts but also redefined the parameters of success in the international realm of the sport. Before Ichiro's arrival on the Major League scene in 2001, there lingered a prevailing skepticism about whether a player from Japan could truly thrive in the highly competitive landscape of Major League Baseball.

Ichiro's entrance into the Major Leagues was not just a chapter in his career but a cultural moment that challenged perceptions. His arrival was met with curiosity, skepticism, and a certain level of uncertainty about how a player from a different baseball tradition would adapt to the rigorous demands of the MLB. However, Ichiro not only adapted; he flourished, surpassing expectations and leaving an indelible mark on the game.

As Ichiro donned the Seattle Mariners uniform, his impact was felt immediately. His exceptional bat speed, unparalleled fielding skills, and trademark slap-hitting style became the talk of the baseball world. But Ichiro brought more than just skill to the plate; he brought a new perspective, a fusion of Eastern and Western approaches to the game that captivated fans and fellow players alike.

In the batter's box, Ichiro's precision and consistency were nothing short of remarkable. He quickly established himself as one of the league's premier hitters, achieving a unique blend of power and finesse. In 2004, he set the MLB single-season record for hits with an astonishing 262—a feat that had stood for over eight decades. His performance earned him not only accolades but also the respect of his peers, erasing any lingering doubts about the ability of a Japanese player to excel in the highest echelons of professional baseball.

Beyond the statistics, Ichiro's impact extended to the broader cultural landscape of the game. He became a symbol of unity, demonstrating that baseball, with its rich traditions, could serve as a bridge connecting players and fans across different continents. Ichiro's success transcended cultural differences, sending a powerful message that talent is a universal language that knows no boundaries.

Ichiro Suzuki's journey was more than a sports story; it was a testament to the power of perseverance, adaptability, and the ability to thrive in unfamiliar environments. His legacy endures not only in the record books but also in the hearts of baseball enthusiasts worldwide. Ichiro's journey opened doors for subsequent generations of Japanese players, and his impact on the cultural tapestry of baseball remains a compelling chapter in the ongoing narrative of the sport.

Toni Stone: Pioneering Women's Baseball in the Negro Leagues

Amidst the backdrop of a segregated America and the dominance of the Negro Leagues, Toni Stone emerged as a trailblazer for women in baseball. Her story, a significant chapter in the history of the sport, unfolded during an era when gender norms and racial prejudices cast formidable shadows over the playing field.

In the year 1953, Toni Stone etched her name into the annals of baseball history as she shattered the gender barrier within the formidable confines of the Negro Leagues. At a time when the sport was predominantly a male domain, Stone's entrance onto the field challenged not only the prevailing gender norms but also confronted the deeply ingrained racial prejudices of the era.

Facing a double-edged sword of discrimination, Toni Stone exhibited unparalleled courage as she stepped up to the plate. Her journey wasn't merely about athletic prowess; it was a testament to resilience and a relentless pursuit of passion in the face of societal barriers. Stone faced skepticism, resistance, and outright hostility, yet her determination remained unyielding.

As the first woman to compete in the esteemed Negro Leagues, Stone became a symbol of defiance against the status quo. Her presence on the field signaled a seismic shift in the perception of women's capabilities in professional baseball. Yet, her journey was far from easy. Stone encountered hostility not just for her gender but also due to the racial dynamics of the time. Segregation and discrimination were pervasive, both on and off the field, but Stone's love for the game propelled her forward.

Toni Stone's legacy extends beyond breaking gender barriers; it is a beacon that illuminates the path for future generations of women who aspire to compete at the highest levels of baseball. Her courage opened doors that were once firmly shut, creating opportunities for others to follow in her footsteps.

In reflecting on Toni Stone's historic achievement, we are reminded that progress often comes in the form of individual courage and determination. Her story serves as a testament to the transformative power of sport, breaking down barriers not only between men and women on the field but also challenging the deeply ingrained racial prejudices of the time. Stone's journey is a reminder that the love of the game knows no gender, and talent, regardless of one's background, deserves its place on the diamond. Her pioneering spirit continues to inspire, urging us to strive for a more inclusive and equitable future in the world of baseball and beyond.

Conclusion: The Enduring Legacy of Inclusion
As we delve into the profound narratives of these trailblazing pioneers who shattered barriers within the realm of baseball, their impact resonates far beyond the mere statistical records. They stand as architects of change, visionaries who dismantled the restrictive walls that confined the sport to narrow demographics. Their journeys were

not just about playing a game; they were about altering the course of history.

The stories of Jackie Robinson, Roberto Clemente, Mo'ne Davis, Ichiro Suzuki, and Toni Stone echo with the resounding notes of a symphony of inclusion. Each swing, pitch, and stolen base became a movement in this symphony, transcending the boundaries of race, gender, and cultural expectations. The collective efforts of these pioneers painted a new narrative for baseball—one that challenged preconceived notions and beckoned us to redefine the very essence of the sport.

Yet, as we stand on the shoulders of these giants, the symphony of inclusion remains unfinished. The echoes of their triumphs inspire us to continue the melody, harmonizing the diverse voices that make up the grand orchestra of baseball. The pioneers did not merely break barriers; they laid the foundation for a more inclusive future, one where talent knows no boundaries, and the field truly becomes a level playing ground for all who cherish the game.

Their legacy is a call to action, urging us to challenge the status quo, foster diversity, and ensure that every aspiring player, regardless of their background, has the opportunity to step onto the hallowed diamond. Breaking barriers is not confined to the pages of history; it is an ongoing narrative that challenges the very fabric of the sport, pushing it to evolve and embrace the richness of its diverse participants.

Through the stories of these trailblazers, young readers are not just invited to dream without limits; they are encouraged to actively shape the future of baseball. The game, once confined by societal norms, is now a canvas upon which dreams are painted in every shade imaginable. The diversity and courage of those who dared to break barriers have not only enriched the game but have become the driving force behind its perpetual evolution.

As the symphony of inclusion plays on, we are reminded that the journey toward true diversity and equality is a collective endeavor. Every swing of the bat, every pitch, and every moment on the field contribute to the melody that continues to redefine what baseball represents. The unfinished symphony beckons us all to become custodians of inclusion, ensuring that the legacy of these pioneers remains not just a part of baseball's history but a guiding light for its future.

Chapter 7: Underdog Stories: Triumphs Against All Odds

In the tapestry of baseball, some of the most compelling stories emerge not from the favored teams but from those that defy the odds stacked against them. This chapter delves into the heartwarming tales of underdog teams and players who, against all expectations, achieved victories that resonated far beyond the baseball diamond.

The Unlikely Contenders: Defying the Odds in Baseball
Within the dynamic landscape of sports, underdog teams are frequently relegated to the role of mere participants, seemingly destined to yield to more formidable opponents. Yet, within the confines of baseball, a sport renowned for its capricious nature, the underdogs carve a narrative that transcends statistical analyses. Their tales unfold as sagas of

unwavering resilience, deep-seated belief, and an unyielding refusal to be bound by preconceived notions.

In the world of baseball, where statistics often paint a predictable picture of success, the underdogs emerge as living testaments to the unpredictable essence of the game. They stand as reminders that the field is not merely a battleground for the favored, but a stage where determination and grit can outshine even the most imposing adversaries.

In the face of statistical disparities, these underdog stories resonate as beacons of inspiration. Unlike tales scripted by numerical advantages, they are narratives defined by the sheer will of players who refuse to accept predetermined outcomes. The essence of baseball lies not just in the empirical evaluation of skills but in the intangible qualities that elevate a team or player beyond the constraints of expectation.

As underdog teams take the field, they carry with them the weight of skepticism, the odds stacked against them like an insurmountable wall. It is within this crucible of doubt that the true character of these teams is revealed. They become architects of their own destiny, shattering the illusions of predetermined defeat and crafting stories that echo through the corridors of baseball history.

The unpredictability inherent in baseball becomes the canvas upon which these underdog narratives unfold. Every pitch, swing, and play becomes a stroke in a masterpiece, illustrating the artistry of perseverance and the tenacity to overcome formidable challenges. The game, with all its uncertainties, becomes a testament to the fact that triumph is not reserved for those with statistical advantages, but for those who dare to defy expectations.

In exploring the stories of underdog triumphs, it becomes evident that the true beauty of baseball lies not just in the final score but in the journey that leads to it. These tales of unexpected victories embody the very spirit of the sport, reminding us that the heart of baseball beats not only in the prowess of statistical dominance but in the resilience and belief that transform unlikely contenders into timeless champions.

The Miracle Season: The '69 Mets - A Defining Chapter in Baseball History

In the rich tapestry of baseball, few tales resonate as profoundly as the story of the 1969 New York Mets—a narrative that stands as a testament to the enduring power of the underdog spirit. It was a season that defied conventional wisdom, turning a team with a history of never experiencing a winning season into a force that not only competed in the World Series but triumphed against all odds.

The Mets, a franchise born in 1962, had known little but disappointment in their early years. They were dubbed the "Lovable Losers," with a track record that seemed to perpetually place them at the bottom of the league. However, the winds of change began to sweep through Shea Stadium in Flushing, Queens, as the 1969 season unfolded.

Led by a cadre of determined players and under the stewardship of manager Gil Hodges, the Mets embarked on a journey that would rewrite their narrative in the annals of baseball lore. The iconic Tom Seaver, a pitching maestro, emerged as the anchor of the team—a beacon of excellence in a season that would be defined by unexpected triumphs.

The regular season witnessed the Mets not only securing a winning record but also clinching the National League East title, a feat that few had anticipated. The stage was set for a clash with the highly favored Baltimore Orioles in the World Series.

Facing a team considered by many as unbeatable, the Mets embraced the underdog role with unwavering determination. The '69 World Series unfolded as a David-and-Goliath tale, with the Mets overcoming the odds to secure a historic victory in five games. Tom Seaver's brilliance on the mound and the timely hitting of players like Cleon Jones and Tommie Agee became the stuff of legends.

The championship parade that followed through the streets of New York marked not only the Mets' triumph but a city's collective celebration of a team that had defied expectations. The Miracle Mets, as they came to be known, transformed the narrative around the franchise and inspired generations of baseball enthusiasts.

The '69 Mets' underdog story resonates not just for its impact on the baseball landscape but for the broader cultural significance it held. In a time marked by societal upheavals, the Mets' improbable journey became a symbol of hope and resilience—a reminder that, even in the face of adversity, victory could be achieved through teamwork, determination, and a belief in the extraordinary. The Miracle Mets etched their place not only in sports history but in the hearts of fans who witnessed the magic of an underdog becoming a champion.

David vs. Goliath: The '88 Dodgers

In the realm of baseball history, the 1988 Los Angeles Dodgers etched an indelible mark as a quintessential underdog team. As they entered the World Series, they found themselves pitted against the formidable Oakland Athletics, a team hailed as baseball juggernauts. What unfolded was a saga of determination, resilience, and a defining moment that would forever be etched in the hearts of baseball enthusiasts.

The Dodgers faced considerable challenges as they entered the World Series, with key players grappling with injuries that threatened to undermine their chances. Yet, adversity became a crucible for unity, and under the guidance of their seasoned leader, the legendary Kirk Gibson, the team embarked on a journey that would captivate the baseball world.

Kirk Gibson, renowned for his tenacity and never-say-die attitude, emerged as the linchpin of the Dodgers' underdog narrative. As a seasoned player, Gibson's leadership on and off the field infused the team with a spirit that transcended statistical probabilities. The stage was set for a showdown that would be remembered as one of the greatest moments in baseball history.

Game 1 of the World Series unfolded as a gripping duel between the Dodgers and the Athletics. With Gibson nursing injuries of his own, his presence on the field was uncertain. The odds seemed insurmountable, but it was in these moments that the true character of an underdog team comes to the forefront.

In a stunning turn of events, Gibson, hobbled by injuries, was called upon to pinch-hit in the bottom of the ninth inning. The tension in the stadium was palpable as he faced the Athletics' formidable closer, Dennis Eckersley. What transpired next would become a defining moment not just for the '88 Dodgers but for the entire history of the sport.

With unwavering determination, Gibson, battling pain and physical limitations, connected with a pitch and sent it soaring into the night. The iconic home run electrified the stadium and resonated far beyond its walls. Gibson's triumphant hobble around the bases became a symbol of the underdog spirit, defying logic and expectations.

The Dodgers went on to win Game 1 and eventually clinched the World Series title, completing a storybook ending to a season marked by adversity. The '88 Dodgers' victory stands as a testament to the unpredictable nature of baseball, where heart, resilience, and an unwavering belief in one's abilities can defy even the most formidable opponents.

As young readers immerse themselves in the tale of the '88 Dodgers, they learn that triumph often arises from the unlikeliest of circumstances. Kirk Gibson's heroic home run becomes more than a sports moment; it becomes a lesson in the extraordinary potential hidden within the underdog narrative, inspiring a generation to embrace challenges and believe in their ability to overcome them.

The Miracle of 2004: Breaking the Curse
In the hallowed history of the Boston Red Sox, the year 2004 stands out as an epochal chapter—a year that not only defied the odds but

shattered an 86-year championship drought that had cast a shadow over the franchise. The Red Sox, facing a seemingly insurmountable burden, found themselves down three games to none against their arch-rivals, the New York Yankees, in the American League Championship Series (ALCS).

The weight of history bore down on the Red Sox as they stood on the precipice of another postseason disappointment. The specter of the "Curse of the Bambino," a supposed hex dating back to the controversial sale of Babe Ruth to the Yankees in 1918, loomed large. Generations of fans had endured heartbreak after heartbreak, with each passing year reinforcing the belief that a championship was an elusive dream.

The Desperate Stand: A Rally for the Ages

Down 3-0 in the ALCS, the Red Sox faced a daunting challenge—no team in baseball history had ever overcome such a deficit in a postseason series. Yet, it was precisely at this juncture that the Red Sox showcased the resilience and tenacity that would define their historic run. In a dramatic reversal, they mounted a spectacular comeback, winning four consecutive games against the Yankees.

The defining moment came in Game 4, where the Red Sox, trailing by a single run in the bottom of the ninth inning, orchestrated a comeback for the ages. Pinch hitter Dave Roberts's daring stolen base set the stage for an RBI single by Bill Mueller, tying the game and paving the way for an extra-inning victory. The Red Sox carried this momentum into subsequent games, sealing their place in history with a stunning triumph over their rivals.

The Improbable Journey Continues: World Series Glory

Having vanquished the Yankees, the Red Sox entered the World Series with a newfound belief and a mission to erase the decades-long championship drought. Facing the St. Louis Cardinals, they continued their remarkable journey, capturing the series in a four-game sweep.

The grand finale unfolded at Busch Stadium in St. Louis, where the Red Sox secured victory in Game 4, clinching their first championship since 1918. The Curse of the Bambino was officially broken, and a jubilant Boston celebrated a long-awaited triumph that transcended the boundaries of sports.

Legacy of Resilience: Lessons from the 2004 Red Sox

The 2004 Boston Red Sox's triumph goes beyond the box scores and pennants; it is a story of unyielding perseverance, the refusal to succumb to the weight of history, and the belief that, even in the face of the most daunting challenges, victory is attainable. This chapter in baseball history serves as a timeless reminder that resilience, tenacity, and unwavering belief can transform the narrative, rewriting the destiny of a team and inspiring generations of fans to dream the impossible.

Individual Triumphs: Unheralded Heroes in the Spotlight
In the mosaic of baseball, the spotlight often gravitates towards team triumphs, but within this dynamic landscape, individual players often emerge as unsung heroes, defying expectations and rewriting the narrative of their own careers. These tales of individual triumphs are not merely stories of statistical achievements but narratives that embody the essence of perseverance and the capricious nature of the game.

The Rookies Who Ignited Brilliance

In the realm of overlooked rookies, some players, dismissed as too green or untested for the grandeur of the Major Leagues, have risen from obscurity to showcase brilliance on the diamond.

Fernando Valenzuela: A Rookie Sensation

Consider the compelling story of Fernando Valenzuela, whose ascent to stardom in 1981 became a beacon of hope for overlooked rookies everywhere. Initially deemed inexperienced for the Major Leagues, Valenzuela, with his unconventional pitching style and unassuming demeanor, not only earned a spot in the Los Angeles Dodgers' rotation but took the league by storm. His unexpected success not only propelled him to immediate stardom but also garnered him the prestigious Rookie of the Year and Cy Young Awards—a remarkable feat for a player once considered too green for the big stage.

Resilience in the Face of Setbacks

Beyond rookies, seasoned players grappling with career setbacks offer tales of resilience that inspire not only those within the sport but anyone facing adversity in their chosen path.

Jim Abbott: Overcoming Limitations

Enter Jim Abbott, a player born without a right hand, whose journey through the Major Leagues stands as a testament to the power of determination. Facing skepticism throughout his career, Abbott not only secured a place in professional baseball but achieved the extraordinary feat of pitching a no-hitter in 1993. His story transcends the realm of sports, becoming a symbol of overcoming physical limitations and proving that exceptional skill knows no bounds.

Lessons from the Overlooked Stars

These individual triumphs illuminate the unpredictable nature of baseball, where unheralded players can transform into luminaries. Their stories resonate not only within the confines of the ballpark but also serve as a source of inspiration for anyone facing doubts or setbacks. As young readers embark on their own journeys, they carry with them the legacy of these overlooked stars, understanding that resilience, perseverance, and an unyielding passion for the game can lead to triumphs that defy all expectations. The unpredictable journey of baseball mirrors the unpredictability of life itself, and within its tales lie invaluable lessons waiting to be embraced.

Crafting Legacies Beyond the Diamond

These overlooked stars do more than defy the expectations of their time; they craft enduring legacies that extend far beyond the white chalk lines of the baseball field. Their stories resonate not just within the confines of the dugout but become echoes of inspiration for individuals facing challenges in various arenas of life.

Roberto Clemente: A Legacy of Humanitarianism

In the tapestry of baseball history, the name Roberto Clemente stands as a testament to the profound impact a player can have both on and off the field. Despite facing racial prejudices in his early career, Clemente's unwavering dedication to the game and his humanitarian efforts left an indelible mark. Beyond his exceptional skills as an outfielder, Clemente's legacy endures through his tireless commitment to charitable work, tragically culminating in his life being lost while delivering aid to earthquake victims in Nicaragua. His story teaches us that greatness is measured not only in runs and hits but also in the positive impact one can have on the world.

Embracing the Unpredictability

In the unpredictable landscape of baseball, where statistics and projections often fall short, these overlooked stars embody the essence of the game's uncertainty. Their journeys inspire us to embrace the unpredictability of life and to see setbacks not as roadblocks but as opportunities for growth.

Yogi Berra: Turning Quirks into Wisdom

Consider the sage wisdom of Yogi Berra, a player whose unconventional approach to language belied the profound insights he offered. Beyond the humorous and often puzzling Yogi-isms, Berra's career spanned 19 seasons, during which he became an 18-time All-Star and won an astonishing 10 World Series championships with the New York Yankees. His story reminds us that success in baseball—and life—is not always predictable, and that sometimes, the most enduring lessons come from the unexpected.

The Rookie Sensation: Fernando Valenzuela

In the spring of 1981, a relatively unknown rookie pitcher named Fernando Valenzuela stepped onto the mound for the Los Angeles Dodgers, capturing the attention of the baseball world in a way that few could have predicted. At the outset, Valenzuela faced skepticism, deemed by some as too inexperienced for the demands of Major League Baseball.

Born in Navojoa, Mexico, Valenzuela had quietly risen through the Dodgers' minor league system, showcasing a unique pitching style that blended precision, flair, and an impressive array of pitches. However, as he made his debut in the major leagues, the expectations were tempered by the notion that he was, after all, just a rookie.

Despite the doubts, Valenzuela's impact was immediate and profound. He opened the 1981 season with an astonishing display of skill, pitching shutouts in his first two starts. What followed can only be described as "Fernandomania." Valenzuela's dominance on the mound, characterized by his unorthodox windup and devastating screwball, captured the imaginations of fans and pundits alike.

Fernandomania transcended the sport itself, becoming a cultural phenomenon. Valenzuela's success wasn't confined to the statistics; it was a symbol of hope and inspiration for millions, particularly within the Mexican-American community. As he continued to excel on the field, Valenzuela's impact reached far beyond the confines of Dodger Stadium.

By the end of the 1981 season, Fernando Valenzuela had amassed a collection of accolades, including the Rookie of the Year and the Cy Young Award. His unexpected success not only propelled him to stardom but also shattered the preconceived notions surrounding rookie pitchers. Valenzuela's journey from an unheralded prospect to a baseball icon showcased the hidden potential within seemingly unremarkable beginnings.

His story serves as a reminder that greatness can emerge from unexpected quarters, that talent and determination can defy conventional expectations. As young readers explore the pages of Valenzuela's chapter, they glimpse into a real-life underdog tale—one that unfolded on the hallowed grounds of a baseball diamond and left an enduring legacy in the hearts of fans and aspiring players alike.

The Resilience of Jim Abbott: Overcoming Physical Odds

In the annals of baseball history, the remarkable journey of Jim Abbott stands as a testament to the indomitable human spirit. Born without a right hand, Abbott faced skepticism and doubters from the early stages of his career. However, his narrative transcends the boundaries of physical limitations, showcasing the extraordinary resilience that propelled him to success in the Major Leagues.

A Unique Beginning

Jim Abbott's story begins with a unique circumstance – a congenital condition that led to his being born without a right hand. From the outset, the odds seemed stacked against him in a sport where intricate coordination and dexterity are paramount. As he pursued his passion for baseball, Abbott encountered raised eyebrows and questions about how he could possibly navigate the complexities of the game without a complete set of limbs.

Rising Above Doubts

Undeterred by skepticism, Abbott honed his skills on the diamond from a young age. His determination and work ethic quickly became apparent, dispelling doubts about his ability to compete at the highest levels. A standout college career at the University of Michigan showcased not only his talent but also his unwavering commitment to the game.

Major League Triumphs

Abbott's journey reached its pinnacle when he entered the Major Leagues, debuting with the California Angels in 1989. The transition from the amateur ranks to professional baseball is challenging for any player, but for Abbott, it carried the added weight of disproving the naysayers who questioned whether he could handle the demands of the sport.

A Pinnacle Achievement: The 1993 No-Hitter
One of the defining moments in Jim Abbott's career occurred on September 4, 1993, while pitching for the New York Yankees. In a dazzling display of skill and fortitude, Abbott achieved a rare and prestigious feat in baseball – he threw a no-hitter against the Cleveland Indians. This remarkable accomplishment silenced critics and reinforced that Abbott's success was not a product of sympathy or tokenism; it was a genuine triumph rooted in talent and resilience.

Beyond Baseball: A Legacy of Inspiration
Jim Abbott's impact extends far beyond the baseball diamond. His story is not just about overcoming physical challenges but about inspiring countless individuals facing adversity in various forms. Abbott's journey exemplifies that success is not limited by external circumstances but is, instead, a reflection of inner strength, perseverance, and an unyielding belief in one's capabilities.

Conclusion: Lessons from Jim Abbott's Journey
Jim Abbott's resilience in the face of doubt and his unparalleled achievements stand as a beacon of inspiration. Young readers are encouraged to reflect on Abbott's story, understanding that obstacles, whether physical or otherwise, can be surmounted with tenacity and belief. As they navigate their own challenges, they carry with them the legacy of a pitcher who defied expectations, proving that the triumph of the human spirit is a narrative that transcends the boundaries of any playing field.

Conclusion: Drawing Wisdom from Underdog Triumphs

In the riveting tapestry of baseball history, the tales of underdog triumphs not only elicit the thrill of victory but also serve as profound repositories of life lessons. Beyond the crack of the bat and the roar of the crowd, these stories embody the essence of resilience, teamwork, and an unyielding belief that even in the face of seemingly insurmountable odds, triumph remains within grasp.

Resilience in the Face of Adversity

The underdog stories showcased in the realm of baseball are living testaments to the power of resilience. When confronted with challenges—be it a losing streak, injuries, or the skepticism of critics—players and teams refused to succumb. Instead, they embraced adversity as a catalyst for growth, proving that setbacks are not permanent roadblocks but rather stepping stones to future success.

Teamwork: The Collective Symphony of Victory

In the symphony of baseball, the underdog tales resound with the harmonious notes of teamwork. Teams comprised of individuals often dismissed as less formidable managed to synchronize their efforts, demonstrating that the collective spirit can overcome the mightiest opponents. These stories underscore the importance of collaboration, communication, and a shared commitment to a common goal—a lesson resonant not only on the field but in the broader arenas of life.

Unwavering Belief as a Driving Force

The unwavering belief that permeates underdog stories is a beacon guiding players through the darkest innings. Whether facing a seasoned adversary or confronting historical droughts, underdogs held onto the conviction that triumph was not a distant dream but an attainable reality. This steadfast belief, often against all rational expectations, became a driving force propelling underdogs to heights previously thought unreachable.

Lessons for the Young and Aspiring
To the young readers who embark on their own journeys, these underdog stories extend an invitation to draw inspiration from the tales of the diamond. Recognize that their paths may be dotted with unexpected victories and seemingly insurmountable challenges. In every setback lies an opportunity for a comeback, a chance to redefine the narrative, and a moment to showcase resilience and determination.

Stepping onto Metaphorical Baseball Fields
As these young enthusiasts step onto their metaphorical baseball fields, they carry with them the indomitable spirit of underdogs who defied the odds. The legacy of those who embraced challenges, fostered teamwork, and held steadfast to their dreams becomes a guiding light. Each swing of the bat, every pitch thrown, and every play made is an opportunity to channel the resilience and belief witnessed in the triumphs of underdog heroes.

In the pages of baseball history, underdog stories stand not only as athletic feats but as living embodiments of the human spirit's capacity to overcome, persevere, and triumph against all odds. As the next generation of players and fans takes their places in the grand narrative of the sport, may they carry forward the enduring legacy of underdogs who, with grit and determination, etched their names into the heart of baseball lore.

Chapter 8:Leadership on and off the Field: Captains and Role Models

In the grand tapestry of baseball, leaders emerge not only for their prowess on the field but also for the positive impact they make beyond the foul lines. This chapter delves into the stories of players celebrated not just for their athletic abilities but for their exceptional leadership qualities and contributions to their communities.

Derek Jeter: A Captivating Leader

In the rich history of baseball, few figures shine as brightly as Derek Jeter, known affectionately as "The Captain." Jeter's legacy extends far beyond the diamond, leaving an indelible mark on the sport through his exemplary leadership, both on and off the field.

As a shortstop and batter, Jeter's exceptional skills are etched into the record books, but it is his leadership that truly sets him apart. His tenure as captain of the New York Yankees is a testament to his ability to unite players, foster camaraderie, and navigate the challenges of a high-stakes, high-pressure sport. Jeter's leadership style is characterized by a quiet confidence, a steadying presence that resonated throughout the clubhouse, and an unwavering commitment to the success of his team.

One of Jeter's defining qualities as a leader was his capacity to perform under pressure, earning him the nickname "Captain Clutch." In crucial moments, when the game hung in the balance, Jeter's poise and determination were catalysts for his team's success. This ability to rise to the occasion solidified not only his standing as a captain but also his place in the hearts of fans who witnessed his heroics time and again.

However, Jeter's leadership extended beyond the confines of the baseball diamond. Off the field, he leveraged his platform to make a positive impact on the lives of young people. Through the Turn 2 Foundation, which he established in 1996, Jeter dedicated himself to fostering leadership skills and academic excellence among youth. The foundation's initiatives include programs that promote healthy lifestyles, academic achievement, and community involvement, reflecting Jeter's commitment to shaping well-rounded individuals beyond the realm of sports.

Jeter's philanthropic efforts are not mere gestures; they are a reflection of his genuine desire to create lasting change. His leadership legacy is one of inspiration, encouraging aspiring athletes to not only excel in their respective sports but also to recognize the broader responsibilities that come with their influence. Through Derek Jeter's story, young readers are invited to explore the multifaceted nature of leadership and understand that true greatness is achieved not only by personal accomplishments but also by the positive impact one leaves on the world.

Roberto Clemente: A Humanitarian Beacon

In the annals of baseball history, few figures shine as brightly off the field as they do on it. Roberto Clemente, a revered Hall of Fame outfielder, left an indelible mark not only for his athletic prowess but for his unwavering commitment to social justice and humanitarian causes.

Clemente's legacy is woven into the fabric of baseball lore, a testament to a life lived with purpose and compassion. Known for his powerful arm and exceptional hitting, he graced the outfield for the Pittsburgh Pirates, becoming a fixture in the hearts of fans for reasons that extended far beyond the diamond.

His leadership, marked by a profound sense of duty to make a positive impact, reached its tragic zenith in December 1972. Responding to the devastating earthquake in Nicaragua, Clemente organized the shipment of aid to the victims. Determined to ensure that the aid reached those in need, he personally accompanied the cargo on a flight. Tragically, the plane crashed, claiming Clemente's life and leaving an irreplaceable void in the baseball community.

Clemente's commitment to humanitarian causes, epitomized by his final act of selflessness, transformed him into a symbol of benevolence and compassion. His legacy, etched not only in his baseball achievements but in the depth of his humanity, stands as a beacon for athletes and individuals alike. His untimely death underscored the profound impact that athletes can have beyond the realm of sports, amplifying their roles as ambassadors for positive change.

Through the Roberto Clemente Award, established by Major League Baseball to honor those who best exemplify the spirit of giving back, his legacy endures. The award serves as a reminder that the spirit of humanitarianism and social responsibility continues to be a vital part of the baseball ethos, inspired by the enduring legacy of a man whose compassion transcended the confines of the baseball diamond. As young readers explore Clemente's story, they are invited not only to appreciate his athletic feats but to consider the profound difference they too can make in the world beyond the game.

Torii Hunter: A Genuine Leader on and off the Diamond
In the illustrious history of baseball, few players embody the essence of leadership with the sincerity and heart that Torii Hunter brought to the game. As a charismatic outfielder, Hunter's impact stretched far beyond his remarkable defensive skills, leaving an enduring legacy that resonated not only on the field but also within the clubhouse and in communities he ardently supported.

Renowned for his exceptional defensive prowess, Torii Hunter's influence extended beyond the statistics recorded on the scorecard. His defensive artistry in the outfield was not merely a demonstration of athleticism but a testament to his dedication to the success of his team. His ability to make awe-inspiring catches and crucial plays was matched only by his unyielding commitment to the principles of teamwork.

Inside the clubhouse, Hunter's presence was transformative. His infectious energy and genuine passion for the game made him a natural leader. Teammates looked up to him not just for his baseball acumen but for the positive atmosphere he cultivated. Whether rallying for a comeback or offering guidance to younger players, Hunter's leadership was marked by authenticity, a quality that resonated with teammates and fans alike.

However, Torii Hunter's impact wasn't confined to the baseball diamond alone. Off the field, he leveraged his stature and influence to make a tangible difference in the lives of others. His involvement in charitable initiatives, particularly those centered around youth and education, underscores his commitment to giving back. Hunter understood the transformative power of education and sought to provide opportunities for young individuals to flourish, both academically and personally.

Through his Torii Hunter Project, he aimed to create positive change by investing in educational programs, scholarships, and community development projects. Hunter's dedication to making a lasting impact on the communities he touched became a defining aspect of his legacy. His charitable endeavors weren't mere gestures; they were a reflection of his deeply ingrained belief in the responsibility of athletes to contribute to the betterment of society.

As young readers delve into Torii Hunter's story, they encounter not just a player with exceptional athletic abilities but a leader whose authenticity, heart, and commitment to community resonate as enduring lessons. His journey illustrates that true leadership extends beyond the boundaries of the baseball field, leaving an indelible mark on the lives of those fortunate enough to be touched by it. In the following chapters, we'll continue to explore the multifaceted nature of baseball, where players not only play the game but also inspire and uplift those around them.

Clayton Kershaw: Catalyst for Change

In the realm of baseball, few names shine as brightly as Clayton Kershaw's. Renowned for his prowess as a dominant left-handed pitcher, Kershaw's impact on the sport extends far beyond the pitcher's mound. However, it is not just his extraordinary pitching statistics that distinguish him; it's his unwavering commitment to philanthropy that truly sets him apart.

Kershaw's journey as a philanthropist takes center stage through his organization, Kershaw's Challenge. Established with his wife, Ellen, this foundation embodies their shared vision to make a tangible and lasting difference in the lives of those in need. The driving force behind Kershaw's philanthropy is a deep-rooted belief that athletes possess a unique platform—one that can be harnessed for social good.

Beyond the confines of Dodger Stadium, Kershaw's Challenge works tirelessly to support various charitable initiatives, with a particular focus on improving the lives of children. From providing education and healthcare resources to empowering underprivileged youth, Kershaw's commitment to philanthropy is both broad and impactful.

The left-handed maestro doesn't merely write checks; he invests time, energy, and genuine compassion into each initiative. Kershaw is often seen actively participating in events, visiting hospitals, and engaging with the communities he aims to uplift. His hands-on approach underscores a leadership style that goes beyond the glamour of the game, exemplifying a genuine desire to effect positive change.

One of Kershaw's signature projects is "Kershaw's Challenge: Arise Africa," a program that focuses on transforming the lives of children in Zambia. The initiative tackles issues such as access to education, healthcare, and nutrition, recognizing that the challenges these children face extend beyond the baseball diamond. Through fundraising events, partnerships, and advocacy, Kershaw's Challenge has become a beacon of hope for countless children and families.

As young readers explore Kershaw's story, they witness the embodiment of a baseball player who not only excels in his craft but leverages his success to impact lives. Clayton Kershaw's journey serves as a poignant reminder that the influence of a sports figure can extend beyond the roar of the crowd, inspiring a sense of responsibility and a commitment to making the world a better place—one pitch at a time.

In the subsequent chapters, we'll continue our exploration of the multifaceted nature of baseball, delving into the passion and love that players bring to the game and discovering the boundless joy that the sport can instill in the hearts of fans.

Leadership Unveiled: The Impact Beyond Statistics
In the realm of baseball, where the relentless pursuit of statistics often dominates the narrative, true leadership extends far beyond the realms of batting averages and earned run averages. Examining the pages of the sport's storied history unveils a collection of leaders who, beyond

their athletic prowess, have left an indelible mark on the hearts of fans and the communities they've touched.

Derek Jeter: A Captain Beyond the Diamond
Derek Jeter, the iconic shortstop and captain of the New York Yankees, exemplifies leadership that transcends mere on-field achievements. Jeter's impact extended to the very fabric of his team, where he served as a unifying force. His influence was not solely measured by the championships he secured but by the intangible qualities of leadership—integrity, resilience, and an unwavering commitment to excellence. Off the field, Jeter's establishment of the Turn 2 Foundation underscored his dedication to education and community empowerment, showcasing that true leadership extends well beyond the chalk lines.

Roberto Clemente: A Humanitarian Beacon
Roberto Clemente, the legendary Pittsburgh Pirates outfielder, stands as a beacon of humanitarianism within the realm of baseball history. His leadership wasn't confined to the outfield; it reverberated in his commitment to social justice causes. Clemente's tragic death while delivering aid to Nicaragua showcased his unwavering dedication to making a tangible impact beyond the diamond. His legacy serves as a poignant reminder that genuine leadership is rooted in compassion and a commitment to the betterment of humanity.

Torii Hunter: Heartfelt Leadership
Torii Hunter, the charismatic outfielder known for his dynamic play and magnetic personality, brought more than just athleticism to the ballpark. As a leader in the clubhouse, Hunter's impact was felt through his authentic connection with teammates and a dedication to fostering a positive team culture. Beyond the bases, Hunter's engagement in

charitable endeavors, particularly those aimed at supporting youth and education, highlighted his belief in using his influence to uplift communities.

Clayton Kershaw: Pitching for a Purpose
Clayton Kershaw, the dominant left-handed pitcher for the Los Angeles Dodgers, emerged not only as a master of the mound but as a leader dedicated to making a positive difference. His philanthropic efforts through Kershaw's Challenge reflect a commitment to addressing social issues and making a lasting impact on the lives of children. Kershaw's leadership is a testament to the idea that athletes can be catalysts for positive change, leveraging their platform for the greater good.

The Ripple Effect of True Leadership
These players, etched into the rich tapestry of baseball history, remind us that leadership is not confined to the statistics that adorn scorecards. Their influence extends like ripples in a pond, reaching fans in the stands and communities beyond the ballpark. Young readers exploring these stories are not just spectators to athletic achievements but witnesses to the profound impact of character, integrity, and the ethos of giving back—essential components that define true leadership.

As we continue our exploration, we'll dive into the heart of the game—the players who embody passion and love for baseball, unveiling the sport as not merely a competition but a wellspring of boundless joy and inspiration for both players and fans alike.

Chapter 9: The Heart of the Game: Passion and Love for Baseball

In the grand tapestry of baseball's storied history, there exists a chapter that transcends statistics, accolades, and championships. It's a chapter that delves into the very essence of the sport—the heartbeat that resonates through the crack of the bat, the roar of the crowd, and the green expanse of the baseball field. This chapter celebrates the players who not only played with skill but with an unmatched passion, revealing the profound joy that baseball brings.

The Harmonious Rhythms of the Diamond

For every aficionado of baseball, the diamond is not merely a playing field—it is a grand stage where a symphony of sights and sounds unfolds in perfect harmony. Picture the scene: the crack of a bat meeting a well-thrown ball, the rhythmic cadence of players engaged in the dugout banter, and the resounding cheer that rises from a crowd bound together by a shared affection for the game. These instances compose the melodic undertones that echo through the soul of baseball, capturing the very essence of this revered sport.

In the realm of the diamond, each play, every pitch, and all the spontaneous interactions contribute to the rich tapestry of this symphony. It's not just a physical contest; it's a sensory experience that engages players and fans alike, transcending the boundaries of mere competition. These are the moments that transcend the physical dimensions of the field, transforming it into a theater of pure, unbridled passion.

As the bat connects with the ball, there's a distinct and resonant percussion—the crisp sound that reverberates through the air, signifying a well-executed play. This auditory punctuation marks not only the success of the hitter but also the culmination of collective effort on the field.

Amidst the strategic plays and skillful maneuvers, the dugout becomes a hub of lively interaction. The rhythmic chatter of teammates, sharing insights, offering encouragement, and strategizing for the next move, contributes to the intricate orchestration of the game. It's a camaraderie that goes beyond the individual brilliance of players, fostering a sense of unity and shared purpose.

However, the true crescendo of this symphony emanates from the stands—the collective cheer of a crowd that forms a community bonded by a deep love for the game. This communal expression, a spontaneous eruption of joy, transcends individual affiliations. Whether rooting for the home team or the visiting challengers, the collective cheer is a manifestation of shared appreciation for the spectacle unfolding on the diamond.

In understanding these elements—the crisp crack of the bat, the rhythmic banter in the dugout, and the collective cheer of the crowd—one grasps the heart of baseball. It's a sport where the synergy of individual talents and collective passion converges, creating a symphony that resonates not only through the stadium but lingers in the memories of those fortunate enough to witness its harmonious performance.

The Joyful Swing: A Legacy of Exuberance

Step into the world of baseball legends whose swings were not mere displays of technical prowess but rather vibrant expressions of unadulterated joy. Beyond the precision and mechanics of their hits, these players infused the game with an infectious enthusiasm that left an indelible mark on the hearts of fans and the history of baseball itself.

The Dance of Triumph

For these exceptional players, the journey around the bases was more than a mere routine—it was a choreography of triumph. Each sprint became a dance of joy, a celebration of success that mirrored the exuberance felt by both player and fan alike. The energy they brought to the bases was not just a display of speed; it was a testament to the pure elation derived from the game they loved.

Leaps of Victory

Home runs were not just statistical achievements for these legends; they were moments of unbridled bliss. Picture the jubilant leaps as they rounded the bases, a physical manifestation of the joy that coursed through their veins. These leaps were not just a display of athleticism; they were a visual representation of the uncontainable excitement that fueled their every play.

Beyond the Diamond
The love for baseball that defined these players wasn't confined to the boundaries of the field. It permeated every aspect of their lives, becoming an integral part of their being. Whether interacting with fans off the field, participating in community events, or simply savoring the camaraderie within the clubhouse, their passion for the game extended far beyond the nine innings of a match.

A Living Legacy
In the annals of baseball history, these joyful players left behind more than records and statistics; they created a legacy that transcends generations. The joy they brought to the game wasn't fleeting—it became an enduring part of the sport's narrative. Their influence is seen not only in the highlight reels but in the smiles of fans who recall their era and in the aspiring players who seek to replicate not just their swings but the joy they brought to the diamond.

The Continued Celebration
As we revisit the tales of these legendary players, it becomes clear that their impact extends far beyond the physical act of swinging a bat. They remind us that baseball is not just about competition; it's a celebration of the sheer joy that comes from playing the game. In every swing, every sprint, and every leap, their spirit lives on, perpetuating the

timeless legacy of exuberance that enriches the very essence of baseball.

The Kid at Heart: Roberto Clemente

In the illustrious history of baseball, few figures stand out as vividly as the legendary Roberto Clemente. Beyond the statistical brilliance that defined his career, Clemente's essence on the field transcended the numbers. His passion for the game not only reverberated through his extraordinary plays but also radiated in the infectious joy he brought to every moment.

Born in Carolina, Puerto Rico, in 1934, Clemente's journey to becoming an icon of the game was marked by talent, resilience, and an unwavering love for baseball. From the moment he first stepped onto a baseball field, his passion was palpable, creating a connection with fans that went beyond the boundaries of the diamond.

Clemente's smile, as iconic as his swing, became a symbol of the joy he derived from the game. It wasn't just a display of happiness after a victory; it was a constant companion, accompanying him through every inning and every at-bat. This infectious joy was a reflection of his genuine love for the sport and his understanding of its profound impact on both players and fans.

His prowess in the outfield showcased not only his athletic prowess but also his unbridled enthusiasm for making extraordinary plays. Whether tracking down a fly ball with grace or unleashing a powerful throw from right field to cut down a runner, Clemente played with a childlike zeal that endeared him to fans and earned the respect of opponents.

Clemente's joyous approach to the game wasn't confined to personal achievements or team victories; it extended to the camaraderie he shared with teammates and the connection he forged with fans. His interactions off the field, whether signing autographs for young admirers or engaging in community initiatives, demonstrated a man who understood the power of baseball to inspire and unite.

His impact reached its pinnacle during the 1971 World Series when he led the Pittsburgh Pirates to victory, earning the MVP title. Beyond the statistics, it was his infectious enthusiasm and unwavering dedication that solidified his place as one of baseball's most beloved figures.

Tragically, Clemente's life was cut short in 1972, but his legacy endures as a testament to the enduring joy that baseball can bring. The Roberto Clemente Award, established in his honor, recognizes players who exemplify sportsmanship, community involvement, and contribution to their teams—a fitting tribute to a man whose passion extended beyond the game itself.

In celebrating Roberto Clemente, we not only acknowledge his athletic prowess but also honor the kid at heart who played the game with boundless joy. His legacy lives on, reminding us that amidst the intensity of competition, the heart of baseball beats with the simple and profound joy that captivates players and fans alike.

Embracing the Game's Quirks: Reveling in Baseball's Unique Charm

Within the realm of baseball, where the pursuit of victory is both noble and relentless, there exists a cadre of players who understand that the sport's beauty lies not only in grand feats but in the subtle nuances that make it an extraordinary tapestry of moments. These players, true custodians of the heart of the game, find joy in the peculiarities and idiosyncrasies that define the baseball experience.

Rituals Before the At-Bat: A Personal Symphony
Step into the batter's box, and you'll find a ritualistic dance of preparation that extends beyond the physical. For many players, the moments before an at-bat are a canvas for personal rituals—a tap of the cleats, a precisely timed series of practice swings, or a heartfelt nod to the heavens. These rituals, seemingly quirky to outsiders, are deeply personal and serve as a rhythmic prelude to the impending battle with the pitcher. They encapsulate a player's connection to the game, an intimate dance that goes beyond the box score.

Camaraderie During Rain Delays: Unveiling Bonds Beyond the Game
When rain disrupts the symphony of a baseball game, an unexpected camaraderie unfolds in the dugouts. Players, usually divided by team allegiances, come together under the shelter, sharing stories, jokes, and even impromptu games to pass the time. These moments of shared laughter and camaraderie during rain delays reveal a profound truth—the bonds forged in the crucible of competition extend beyond the field. It's a reminder that, amidst the pursuit of victory, there's a shared love for the game that transcends rivalries.

The Unspoken Language of Baseball: Signs and Gestures
In the intricate ballet of a baseball game, signs and gestures become an unspoken language. From catchers signaling pitches to infielders orchestrating defensive strategies, this silent communication adds a layer of intrigue and strategy to the sport. Players who embrace these subtleties revel not only in the strategic advantage it provides but in the

deep connection it forges between teammates. It's a nod, a wink, a secret language that binds players together in the pursuit of a common goal.

The Oddities of Baseball Stadiums: A Playground of Quirks
Baseball stadiums, each with its own character and quirks, become a playground for players who appreciate the unique charm of each venue. Whether it's the Green Monster at Fenway Park, the ivy-covered walls of Wrigley Field, or the outfield pool in Arizona, these distinctive features add a layer of personality to the game. Players who revel in these quirks understand that the stadium is not just a battleground; it's a canvas that paints a different picture in every city.

A Celebration of the Everyday: Finding Joy in the Routine
Beyond the headline-making plays and dramatic victories, the heart of the game beats in the everyday routines of baseball. From the simple act of stretching before a game to the shared meals after, players who truly embody the essence of baseball find joy in the routine. It's a celebration of the mundane, a recognition that the joy of the game extends far beyond the extraordinary moments to encompass the fabric of daily life in the world of baseball.

In the intricate dance between players and the sport they love, these quirks become the threads that weave a rich tapestry. As we peel back the layers of baseball's peculiar charm, we discover that the heartbeat of the game is not only in the victories but in the moments that make it an enchanting, unpredictable, and endlessly cherished experience.

The Joyful Journey: Ichiro Suzuki's Artistry in Baseball

In the early years of the 21st century, a transcendent figure emerged in Major League Baseball, hailing not from the traditional baseball powerhouses of the United States but from the baseball-loving nation of Japan—Ichiro Suzuki. His journey to the Major Leagues wasn't just a migration; it was a testament to the universal language of baseball and the joy that could be found in its purest form.

Born on October 22, 1973, in Kasugai, Aichi, Japan, Ichiro demonstrated an early affinity for the sport, honing his skills on the baseball diamonds of his homeland. His journey to the Major Leagues began with a historic decision to leave the Orix BlueWave of the Japanese Pacific League, where he had already established himself as one of the league's premier players.

In 2001, at the age of 27, Ichiro Suzuki crossed the Pacific to join the Seattle Mariners, marking the beginning of a chapter that would redefine the expectations of international players in Major League Baseball.

A Symphony of Style and Substance

Ichiro's impact was immediate and profound. His style of play was a unique blend of elegance and efficiency, a symphony of skill and finesse that captured the hearts of fans around the world. As he stepped into the batter's box, his at-bats were meticulous, each swing a brushstroke on the canvas of the game. His ability to consistently put the ball in play and his remarkable speed on the basepaths turned routine plays into thrilling moments.

Graceful Fielding: An Artistic Display

In the outfield, Ichiro's fielding was a testament to his athleticism and spatial awareness. His graceful movements and keen instincts transformed routine catches into balletic performances. The fluidity with which he tracked down fly balls and executed precise throws demonstrated not only his physical prowess but also his deep understanding of the nuances of the game.

The Infectious Smile: A Symbol of Joy

Beyond the statistics and highlight-reel plays, Ichiro's infectious smile became a symbol of the joy he derived from playing baseball. Whether celebrating a hit, making a spectacular play, or interacting with fans, his genuine enthusiasm resonated with audiences and opponents alike. It wasn't just about winning games for Ichiro; it was about relishing every moment on the field.

A Maestro Conducting Brilliance

Ichiro Suzuki wasn't just a player; he was a maestro conducting a symphony of baseball brilliance. His impact extended beyond the box score, influencing the way the game was perceived and played. The success he achieved in the Major Leagues paved the way for a new generation of Japanese players to pursue their dreams on the international stage.

Ichiro's legacy is etched not only in the record books, where he amassed over 3,000 hits in Major League Baseball, but also in the hearts of fans who witnessed his artistry on the diamond. His journey exemplifies the joy that can be found in the pursuit of excellence, the embrace of cultural diversity, and the universal love for the game of baseball.

As young players embark on their own journeys, they can draw inspiration from Ichiro Suzuki's joyful approach to the sport, understanding that in every swing, every catch, and every smile lies the enduring beauty of baseball.

Inspiring the Next Generation: A Legacy of Passion
In the vast stadium of baseball history, the players who transcend the realm of statistics and competition become more than mere athletes—they become mentors and inspirations for the aspiring ballplayers of tomorrow. Their passion for the game isn't just evident in their plays but becomes a powerful message that echoes beyond the confines of the field.

These players, often heralded as stars, emerge as beacons of inspiration for the next generation of ballplayers. Their dedication and love for the game convey a profound lesson: that the heart of baseball lies not solely in the numbers or the thrill of competition, but in the enduring love and joy it brings to all those who step onto the diamond.

In real-life tales of baseball greatness, players like Roberto Clemente and Ichiro Suzuki stand as living monuments to this philosophy. Their on-field exploits were not merely displays of skill but reflections of a genuine passion for the sport. Clemente, with his infectious smile and unwavering love for the game, inspired generations with his joyous approach to every play. Similarly, Ichiro Suzuki's meticulous craftsmanship and graceful demeanor on the field demonstrated that the true essence of baseball extends beyond victories and losses—it resides in the unbridled joy that the game imparts.

The impact of these players extends far beyond the chalk lines of the baseball diamond. Through their actions, they instill in young minds the understanding that baseball is more than a game; it is a source of inspiration and a wellspring of joy. The message is clear: every swing, every catch, and every step taken on the field should be a celebration of the intrinsic love for the sport.

Young readers are encouraged to embrace this philosophy, recognizing that their journey in baseball is not solely defined by wins or losses. Whether basking in the glow of victory or weathering the storms of defeat, the enduring love for baseball remains a constant companion. It is this love that fosters resilience, instills discipline, and shapes character—a lesson that extends beyond the diamond into the broader tapestry of life.

Aspiring ballplayers are urged to find their own joy in the game, to appreciate the camaraderie, the unique moments, and the simple pleasures that baseball offers. The legacy of passion passed down by these players is an invitation for each young athlete to carve their own mark on the sport, not just as participants but as torchbearers of the everlasting love for the game. In the hands of the next generation, the heart of baseball continues to beat with the rhythm of passion, echoing through the ages.

Conclusion: The Enduring Symphony of Baseball
As we stand at the intersection of history and the present, the celebration of players who infused the diamond with their passion and

love for baseball echoes like a timeless melody. Their stories are not just anecdotes from the past but resonant chords that vibrate in the hearts of aspiring ballplayers, creating a symphony that continues to captivate generations.

The symphony of the game extends beyond the confines of the field, reaching into the very essence of what makes baseball a cherished pursuit. It is a celebration of the undying passion that players bring to every swing, every catch, and every moment on the field. The diamond, once a stage for legends, now serves as a canvas where the joy of baseball is painted anew by each player who steps up to the plate.

The enduring heartbeat of baseball lies in the genuine love for the sport, an emotion that transcends eras and connects players across generations. It is a heartbeat that reverberates in the carefully crafted swings of Roberto Clemente, in the precision and artistry of Ichiro Suzuki, and in the collective cheers of fans who understand that baseball is not just a sport but a source of everlasting joy.

For aspiring ballplayers, the legacy of these passionate players is a roadmap, guiding them toward a deeper understanding of the game. It's an acknowledgment that beyond the statistics and the victories, baseball is a journey marked by the unyielding commitment to a craft that brings joy to players and spectators alike.

As the symphony of the game continues, played by those who comprehend its profound beauty, may every swing carry the weight of history and the thrill of possibility. May every catch be a tribute to the countless moments of brilliance that came before. And may every instance on the field be a celebration of the enduring heartbeat of baseball—a heartbeat sustained by the unwavering passion that makes it the beloved game we cherish. The players may change, but the symphony persists, a testament to the everlasting magic that is baseball.

Chapter 10: Learning from Defeat: Turning Setbacks into Success

In the intricate tapestry of baseball, defeat is an inevitable thread woven into the journey of every player. Yet, it is not the defeat itself that defines a player, but rather how they rise from its ashes, transforming setbacks into the fuel for future success. This chapter delves into the stories of remarkable players who, in the face of adversity, turned defeat into a powerful catalyst for triumph.

Roberto Clemente: Triumph through Trials

In the rich tapestry of baseball lore, the saga of Roberto Clemente stands as a testament to unwavering determination and resilience. Born in Carolina, Puerto Rico, Clemente's journey to becoming a baseball legend was a symphony of triumphs and tribulations.

In his formative years as a young player in Puerto Rico, Clemente faced skepticism about his potential to compete at the highest level. The doubts that surrounded him were not mere whispers but echoing sentiments challenging his ability to break through barriers. The prevailing notion was that a player from Puerto Rico might not ascend to the pinnacles of Major League Baseball.

Despite these challenges, Clemente's resolve remained unbroken. Every naysayer, every setback, served not as a deterrent but as fuel for his unwavering commitment to proving his mettle on the field. His journey began to transcend the diamond, evolving into a quest to defy not only baseball norms but also societal expectations.

The turning point in Clemente's narrative unfolded when he joined the Pittsburgh Pirates in 1955. The shift from the sun-soaked fields of Puerto Rico to the vibrant cultural landscape of Pittsburgh presented challenges that extended beyond the baseball diamond. Adjusting to a new culture and facing initial struggles on the field marked a phase in his career that could have easily led to despair.

However, Clemente was not one to succumb to disappointment. Instead, he saw each challenge as an opportunity for growth. Imbued with an insatiable thirst for improvement, he immersed himself in the intricacies of the game. Day in and day out, he honed his skills, refining his batting, perfecting his outfield prowess, and becoming a beacon of dedication for aspiring players.

As the echoes of doubt began to fade, Clemente's emergence as one of the greatest outfielders in baseball history became inevitable. His combination of power, precision, and grace in the outfield was a sight to behold, earning him accolades and admiration. The arc of his career culminated in two World Series championships with the Pittsburgh Pirates and a litany of individual awards, including the National League Most Valuable Player in 1966.

Beyond the statistics and accolades, Clemente's legacy reverberates through his humanitarian efforts. His tragic death in 1972, while en route to deliver aid to earthquake victims in Nicaragua, solidified him as a symbol of compassion and selflessness.

Roberto Clemente's story is not just a chapter in baseball history but a timeless narrative of resilience, determination, and the transformative power of the human spirit. His journey from the sun-drenched fields of Puerto Rico to the exalted heights of baseball greatness is an inspiration for all who face doubt and adversity. Clemente's legacy lives on, etched into the very soul of the sport he graced with his unwavering passion and unparalleled skill.

Jackie Robinson: Pioneering Equality on the Baseball Diamond

In a historic moment that would echo through the corridors of time, Jackie Robinson shattered the racial barriers of Major League Baseball, forever changing the complexion of the sport. His entry into the league marked not only a personal triumph but a seismic shift toward inclusivity in a game that had long been marred by segregation.

Jackie Robinson's journey, however, was far from a walk in the park. Instead, it was a relentless march against the currents of prejudice, racial taunts, and systemic discrimination that pervaded the baseball landscape. The weight of being a trailblazer rested heavily on his shoulders, as he understood that his success would reverberate far beyond the confines of the baseball diamond.

Amidst the adversity, Robinson's response was not one of resignation but of unwavering determination. Each racial epithet, each challenge, became a stepping stone for progress. Rather than letting the negativity consume him, he channeled it into a force for change. The baseball field, once a battleground for racial bias, transformed into a platform for dismantling deeply entrenched prejudices.

Robinson's ability to navigate the minefield of adversity showcased not only his athletic prowess but also his resilience in the face of immense pressure. He stood tall as a symbol of hope, a living testament to the idea that the color of one's skin should never determine one's place on the field or in society.

Through his unparalleled perseverance, Robinson achieved not only personal success but also laid the groundwork for future generations of Black players. He became a beacon of inspiration, a catalyst for the gradual dismantling of discriminatory barriers that had plagued the sport for far too long.

Jackie Robinson's legacy extends beyond statistics and records; it is a testament to the enduring power of courage and determination. His journey exemplifies the transformative potential of an individual who, in the face of adversity, emerges not just as an athlete but as a force for societal change. As young readers explore Robinson's story, they witness the indomitable spirit that turned setbacks into a resounding victory for equality on the baseball diamond and beyond.

Clayton Kershaw: Triumph Beyond the Regular Season

In the illustrious career of Clayton Kershaw, marked by three Cy Young Awards and numerous accolades, there exists a chapter that illustrates the profound resilience of a player when faced with playoff challenges. Kershaw, despite his dominance in the regular season, encountered a narrative that threatened to overshadow his brilliance when the postseason arrived.

The heightened expectations accompanying Kershaw's playoff appearances became a storyline unto itself. The discrepancy between his remarkable regular-season performances and perceived struggles in the postseason became a focal point of discussion within baseball circles. Critics argued that his legacy was at stake, and the weight of these expectations loomed large.

Rather than succumbing to the pressure or letting the narrative define him, Kershaw approached his playoff challenges with a meticulous determination. Understanding that growth often arises from adversity, he dissected his setbacks with a keen analytical eye. Kershaw, known for his precision on the mound, applied that same precision to his self-analysis.

In the crucible of postseason baseball, Kershaw refined his approach. He worked tirelessly to strengthen his mental fortitude, knowing that success in October required not just physical prowess but an unyielding mindset. The adjustments he made were not merely mechanical; they were a testament to a player willing to evolve, to learn from defeat, and to rewrite his narrative on the grandest stage.

The turning point came when Kershaw, armed with newfound resilience, emerged as a force in the postseason. His performances were a testament to both his individual growth and his capacity to elevate his team. In a culmination of determination, the Los Angeles Dodgers, under Kershaw's leadership, secured a historic World Series victory.

Kershaw's journey transcends the diamond, offering a lesson to young readers that even the most accomplished players face challenges. It teaches that true greatness is not measured solely by regular-season accolades but by the ability to confront adversity, adapt, and thrive when the stakes are highest. The narrative surrounding Kershaw's postseason struggles transformed into one of triumph, reinforcing the idea that setbacks can be a catalyst for extraordinary success. His story stands as a beacon, reminding aspiring players that growth is a continuous process, and true champions emerge not in spite of challenges but because of them.

Lisa Fernandez: A Triumph Amidst Softball's Toughest Challenges
In the realm of softball, few names shine as brightly as Lisa Fernandez, a living legend whose journey embodies the resilience and triumph born from adversity. Her story unfurls against the backdrop of the Olympic stage, where she faced the formidable task of representing the United States in the 2000 Olympics following a disheartening loss in the 1996 games.

The disappointment of the 1996 Olympic defeat could have been a crushing blow to many athletes, but not to Lisa Fernandez. Instead of succumbing to the weight of defeat, she harnessed it as a catalyst for transformation. Fernandez recognized the need for change, not only in her approach to the game but also in her personal commitment to excellence.

Undeterred by setbacks, Fernandez initiated a profound overhaul of her training regimen. Tirelessly refining her skills, she exhibited an unparalleled dedication to the craft. Her commitment extended beyond the field, permeating every facet of her preparation. Fernandez's relentless pursuit of perfection became a beacon of inspiration for her teammates and a symbol of the unwavering spirit required to triumph at the highest level.

As the 2000 Olympics dawned, Lisa Fernandez emerged not just as a player but as a leader. Her resilience, honed through the crucible of defeat, defined her approach on the mound and in the dugout. Fernandez's strategic brilliance and unwavering determination propelled the U.S. softball team to a historic gold medal victory.

Beyond the confines of the diamond, Lisa Fernandez's journey serves as a compelling illustration that setbacks are not stumbling blocks but rather stepping stones to greatness. Her story resonates as a testament to the transformative power of perseverance and hard work—a narrative etched not only in the annals of softball history but also in the broader spectrum of athletic achievement.

In the saga of Lisa Fernandez, young readers find a compelling narrative that transcends sports, offering a lesson in resilience, adaptability, and the unyielding spirit required to turn setbacks into triumphs. As they absorb Fernandez's tale, they grasp the profound truth that greatness is not achieved through the absence of challenges but through the tenacity to overcome them, forging a legacy that extends far beyond the boundary lines of any softball field.

Conclusion: Insights Forged in the Diamond

As we delve into the rich narratives of Clemente, Robinson, Kershaw, and Fernandez, a profound theme emerges—one of resilience and transformation in the crucible of defeat. These athletes confronted adversity with a tenacity that defined not only their careers but also their characters. Their stories provide a tangible roadmap for turning setbacks into stepping stones, embodying the spirit of triumph in the realm of sports and beyond.

Roberto Clemente: A Resolve Forged in Doubt

Roberto Clemente's journey reflects a profound resilience that took root in the face of doubt. From his early years in Puerto Rico to the challenges of a new culture in Pittsburgh, every setback became a catalyst for growth. His response to adversity was not merely to endure but to excel. Through meticulous dedication, Clemente transformed criticism into fuel, emerging not just as a formidable player but as a symbol of unwavering determination.

Jackie Robinson: Breaking Chains, Igniting Change

Jackie Robinson's experience shattered barriers and confronted prejudice head-on. The racism he endured on and off the field could have overwhelmed him, yet Robinson turned each negative encounter into an opportunity for societal change. His story underscores that triumph over adversity is not just a personal victory but a force capable of breaking down entrenched norms, paving the way for future generations.

Clayton Kershaw: Mastering the Playoffs

In the realm of baseball, few challenges rival the intensity of postseason play. Clayton Kershaw faced scrutiny for perceived playoff struggles, yet he confronted this narrative with a determination to evolve. Through meticulous self-reflection and a commitment to improvement, Kershaw transformed setbacks into a narrative of postseason dominance. His journey teaches young athletes the transformative power of acknowledging weaknesses and actively working towards growth.

Lisa Fernandez: Gold Forged in Defeat

Lisa Fernandez's journey in softball culminated in the 2000 Olympics, a redemption story built on the foundation of a prior defeat. Her resilience after a disappointing 1996 Olympics showcases the transformative nature of setbacks. Fernandez's commitment to refining her skills and adapting her approach led to a historic gold medal victory, exemplifying that defeat can be a crucible for greatness.

A Lesson for the Aspiring Athlete

This chapter serves as a profound reminder for young readers: defeat, rather than a dead-end, is a pivotal juncture in the journey towards success. These stories exemplify that setbacks are not indicators of failure but rather the bedrock of invaluable lessons. The true measure of a player is not solely in victories but in the ability to rise, evolve, and triumph in the face of adversity.

In the crucible of the diamond, where the echoes of challenges resonate, each setback becomes a chisel carving the path to greatness. These athletes have etched their stories onto the pages of sports history, not just through victories but through their ability to transform defeats into moments of growth, forging characters that stand as beacons of inspiration for aspiring athletes. The diamond, with its trials and triumphs, becomes a forge where the resilience of the human spirit is shaped and honed.

Chapter 11: Conclusion - The Legacy of Baseball

As we round the bases of this journey through inspirational baseball stories, it's essential to reflect on the collective wisdom woven into the fabric of the sport. Each tale has left an indelible mark, not just on the players who lived them but on the essence of baseball itself. In this conclusion, we distill the key lessons from these stories, aiming to inspire young readers to carry the legacy of baseball into their own lives.

The Power of Perseverance

From Alex Rodriguez's humble beginnings to the underdog triumphs on the field, the resounding theme is perseverance. Baseball teaches us that setbacks are not the end but rather the opportunity for a remarkable comeback. Young readers, take note: every strikeout, every missed catch, is a chance to refine your skills and emerge stronger in the face of adversity.

The Triumph of Teamwork

In the chapter on teamwork and camaraderie, we witnessed how victories are sweeter when shared. Baseball teaches us that individual talent is essential, but the real magic happens when players come together as a team. Young players, remember that your success is intertwined with the success of your teammates. Support one another, celebrate victories together, and navigate defeats as a united front.

Embracing Challenges

The stories of players who faced injuries and setbacks underscore a crucial lesson: challenges are an integral part of the game and life. Baseball teaches us not to fear challenges but to embrace them as opportunities for growth. Young readers, when faced with adversity, channel the resilience of these players. Approach challenges with determination, knowing that each obstacle is a stepping stone to success.

Making a Difference Beyond the Field

Baseball is not just a game; it's a platform for making a positive impact beyond the field. Players like Roberto Clemente and Jackie Robinson showed us the profound influence athletes can have on society. Young readers, consider how you can contribute to your community. Whether big or small, your actions can make a difference.

Breaking Barriers and Fostering Inclusivity

The chapter on breaking barriers reminds us that diversity is a strength, and inclusivity is paramount. Baseball has the power to unite people from all walks of life. Young players, be inclusive, challenge stereotypes, and celebrate the richness that diversity brings to the game and the world.

Leadership and Role Modeling

Leadership extends beyond the field, and players like Derek Jeter exemplify this. Baseball teaches us the importance of leading with integrity, humility, and a commitment to the greater good. Young leaders, whether on the field or in your community, strive to be role models who inspire and uplift those around you.

Playing with Passion

The heart of the game lies in the passion players bring to the field. From the little leagues to the major leagues, baseball teaches us to play with joy and enthusiasm. Young players, let the love for the game fuel your efforts. Remember that, in the end, the memories created and the bonds forged are as important as the victories.

Learning from Defeat

Baseball's lessons extend beyond wins and losses. The stories of players who turned defeat into success emphasize the transformative power of resilience. Young readers, view defeats not as failures but as opportunities to learn, grow, and come back stronger.

Carrying the Legacy Forward

As we conclude this exploration of inspirational baseball stories, young readers, consider yourselves keepers of a legacy. The lessons of perseverance, teamwork, embracing challenges, making a difference, breaking barriers, leadership, playing with passion, and learning from defeat are not just for the diamond but for life.

In the vast expanse of baseball history, each player's story has added a unique thread to the rich tapestry of the sport. As you step onto your own fields of dreams, remember that the legacy of baseball is not confined to a game played with a bat and ball—it's a legacy of character, resilience, and the belief that triumph awaits those who dare to dream.

May you carry these lessons with you, young players, and may your journeys be filled with the same passion, determination, and joy that define the heart of baseball. The legacy lives on in each crack of the bat, each cheer from the stands, and in the spirit of every player who has ever taken the field. Play on, and may your stories be the next chapters in the enduring legacy of baseball.